Decarbonising Urban Mobility with Land Use and Transport Policies

THE CASE OF AUCKLAND, NEW ZEALAND

OECD
BETTER POLICIES FOR BETTER LIVES

Please cite this publication as:
OECD (2020), *Decarbonising Urban Mobility with Land Use and Transport Policies: The Case of Auckland, New Zealand*, OECD Publishing, Paris, *https://doi.org/10.1787/095848a3-en*.

ISBN 978-92-64-90322-7 (print)
ISBN 978-92-64-70077-2 (pdf)
ISBN 978-92-64-70069-7 (HTML)
ISBN 978-92-64-95543-1 (epub)

Photo credits: Cover © ssguy/Shutterstock.com

Corrigenda to publications may be found on line at: *www.oecd.org/about/publishing/corrigenda.htm*.

Foreword

Reducing greenhouse gas emissions from urban transport is fundamental to deliver on the Paris Agreement and the Sustainable Development Goals relating to climate change and air quality. Decarbonising urban mobility must be placed at the core of climate change mitigation efforts, as a considerable share of total greenhouse gas emissions originate from the use of private vehicles and other carbon-intensive modes of transport in cities. We are at a critical juncture, as urban populations continue to grow and remain largely dependent on polluting private vehicles.

Given the urgency of the call to action on climate change, a series of important questions seek clear answers. To what extent will technological progress enable reductions in emissions from urban transport? Which land use and transport policies are effective in further reducing emissions? How should governments align these urban policies with relevant national policies, such as fuel taxes? These questions are pressing, as we enter a crucial period that will determine the extent of our transition to a low-carbon economy.

Decarbonising Urban Mobility with Land Use and Transport Instruments: The Case of Auckland supports policy makers in the pursuit of zero carbon urban transport. It is the first OECD report that uses state-of-the-art spatial modelling techniques, which were developed in-house, to evaluate the various impacts of public policies at the urban level. The report projects transport-related greenhouse gas emissions in the city of Auckland, as well as housing prices, public revenue and overall well-being, between 2019 and 2050.

Efforts to decarbonise urban mobility should leverage both transport and land use policies, as transport systems shape urban development and land use patterns have important implications for the environmental performance of urban transport systems. Thus, the development of the appropriate policy mix requires in-depth knowledge of the outcomes of these policies and the interactions between them. The analysis in this report indicates that the transition to zero carbon urban transport will not occur by 2050 without significant policy interventions. In the absence of major policy changes, per capita greenhouse gas emissions will fall but total greenhouse gas emissions from urban road transport will continue increasing, along with urban population and *per capita* income.

The case of Auckland shows that the use of transport policies that promote public transport and electric vehicles, combined with land use policies that foster a more compact urban form, can substantially reduce *per capita* greenhouse gas emissions. Notably, the study finds that increasing the cost of car use, while subsidising public transport fares and electric vehicle purchases, yields positive and significant welfare gains.

Land use policies also play an important role in curbing transport-related greenhouse gas emissions in urban areas characterised by low-density development. The report explores how urban densification can shorten trip distances and lower car dependency, thereby reducing emissions and increasing housing affordability.

While this report focuses on the case of Auckland, the lessons drawn hold wider significance. In particular, the findings are relevant for numerous urban areas in OECD countries that share certain key characteristics with Auckland. Such features include low population density, fragmented public transport networks, a high level of car dependency and high rates of private vehicle ownership. This report helps decision makers understand the implications of policy inaction, as well as anticipate the potential impacts of environmental policies with regard to environmental effectiveness, economic efficiency and social cohesion. More broadly, the conclusions drawn from this study underline the benefit of designing policies in a holistic manner, to leverage their synergies and maximise their effectiveness over multiple domains. The OECD stands ready to assist governments in designing and delivering environmentally effective and economically efficient urban policies that will lead to a better quality of life in cities.

Acknowledgements

This report is an output of the OECD Environmental Policy Committee and its Working Party on Integrating Environmental and Economic Policies (WPIEEP). The report was carried out under the overall responsibility of Shardul Agrawala, Head of the Environment and Economy Integration Division in the OECD Environment Directorate.

All chapters of the report were authored by Ioannis Tikoudis, Tobias Udsholt and Walid Oueslati of the OECD Environment Directorate. Walid Oueslati co-ordinated and oversaw the work on the report. The individual inputs of the key contributors are as follows:

Ioannis Tikoudis	Conceptual design of MOLES, development of MOLES 1.1 software (Auckland version), model calibration and simulations, drafting, data collection and processing, statistical analysis, GIS data analysis and visualisation and communication with stakeholders.
Tobias Udsholt	Drafting, data collection and processing, statistical analysis, GIS data analysis and visualisation and communication with stakeholders.
Walid Oueslati	Project co-ordination and supervision, conceptual design of MOLES, drafting, data collection and communication with stakeholders.

The authors would like to Alexandros Dimitropoulos for his valuable suggestions and Katherine Farrow for her careful and detailed comments on earlier drafts of the report. Further, useful comments and suggestions were received from delegates to the OECD Working Party on Integrating Environmental and Economic Policies (WPIEEP). The authors also owe thanks to OECD colleagues who participated in internal OECD seminars, offered suggestions on the development of MOLES software, or provided feedback on the model and the results of the study. These include Abel Schumann, Willem Adema, Luiz De Mello, Peter Hoeller, Boris Cournede and Åsa Johansson. Other OECD colleagues who provided input on various aspects of the modelling framework and the conclusions of the report include Jean Chateau, Joaquim Oliveira Martins, Rudiger Ahrend, Sebastian Barnes and Arnaud Atoch.

The OECD gratefully acknowledges the support and input provided by the New Zealand Ministry for the Environment and Auckland Council. Multiple other stakeholders, including Auckland Transport, New Zealand Ministry of Transport, New Zealand Transport Authority, New Zealand Ministry of Business, Innovation & Employment, New Zealand Ministry of Housing and Urban Development and the New Zealand Treasury have also facilitated the study by providing data and offering useful input. Feedback and comments from Simon Upton (New Zealand Parliamentary Commissioner for the Environment), Mike Warnock (Auckland Council), and Tamara Linnhoff (New Zealand delegate to WPIEEP) are gratefully acknowledged. The authors especially acknowledge the contribution of Edward Hearnshaw (former New Zealand delegate to WPIEEP), who organised the OECD mission to New Zealand and provided instrumental support to the work in its initial stages.

This report is part of the OECD Spatial Planning Instruments and the Environment (SPINE) project. The SPINE project investigates the role played by spatial planning and land use policies in managing the trade-offs between environmental, economic and social objectives.

Table of Contents

Tables

Figures

Abbreviations and acronyms

BAU	Business as Usual
CBD	Central Business District
CO_2e	Carbon Dioxide
CO_2e	Carbon Dioxide Equivalent
ETS	Emissions Trading Scheme
EV	Electric Vehicle
GHG	Greenhouse Gas
GIS	Geographic Information System
ICE	Internal Combustion Engine
ITF	International Transport Forum
LINZ	Land Information New Zealand
MOLES	Multi-Objective Local Environment Simulator
MoT	Ministry of Transport
NZD	New Zealand Dollars
NZTA	New Zealand Transport Agency
PT	Public Transport
R&D	Research and Development
SDG	Sustainable Development Goal
TD	Targeted Densification
U-CGE	Urban Computable General Equilibrium
VAT	Value Added Tax
WD	Widespread Densification

Executive summary

Cities are home to over half the world's population and their rapid growth is projected to continue. Currently, cities are responsible for 70% of global greenhouse gas emissions and this share will increase as the world becomes increasingly urban (C40, 2019[1]). This makes climate action at the city-level critical to limiting the rise in global average temperature.

Reducing greenhouse gas emissions will require "rapid and far-reaching" changes to consumption and mobility patterns and to the structure of modern economies (IPCC, 2018[1]). The transport sector represents a particular challenge for emission reductions. As incomes and population have grown, emissions from transport have risen faster than in any other sector. Global emissions from road transport alone increased by 77% between 1990 and 2016 (IEA, 2018[2]). Despite rising sales of electric vehicles in recent years, almost all transport activity remains reliant on fossil-fuel powered internal combustion engines. This also holds true in urban environments, where one third of total emissions in major cities is generated by transport (C40, 2019[3]). In the face of growing urban populations, reducing emissions from transport represents a formidable challenge for cities.

This report assesses the impact of demographic and technological changes on emissions from urban transport in Auckland, New Zealand by 2050. The study uses the OECD's integrated land use and transport model, MOLES, to evaluate different land use and transport policies. This modelling framework allows the identification of possible trade-offs between the environmental performance and welfare effects of these policies. Moreover, the model addresses synergies between land use and transport policy instruments.

Auckland is a representative example of a medium-sized city facing challenges in reducing emission from urban transport due to a growing population, low density and high levels of car dependency. The findings are therefore relevant not only to the city of Auckland and New Zealand, but more broadly for the assessment of different pathways to reduce emissions from urban transport in similar contexts.

The report assesses how policies can reduce emissions from the transport sector through three channels:

1. Increasing the share of cleaner forms of transport by encouraging a shift from private vehicles to public transport, biking or walking. Policy options to shift mobility towards cleaner modes include road pricing, per-kilometre taxes and public transport subsidies.
2. Reducing the emissions intensity per kilometre travelled through measures that encourage shifts from fossil-fuel powered cars to electric vehicles. Such measures include incentives and tax exemptions, which favour electric vehicles.
3. Reducing the total number of kilometres travelled by encouraging fewer and shorter trips. Adjusting land use policies, such as maximum density restrictions, can be key to reducing total distances travelled.

Key findings:

- **In the reference scenario, total annual CO_2 emissions from road transport in Auckland are projected to increase by 7% in 2050, relative to 2018 emissions.** This increase will take place despite a number of trends that will reduce *per capita* CO_2 emissions from urban transport in Auckland by 40% over the same time period. These trends include projected improvements in the energy efficiency of vehicles, declining costs of electric vehicles and accompanying increase in EV ownership, a less carbon-intensive electricity sector and the electrification of public transport. Therefore, in the presence of a growing population, technological and other developments will be insufficient to reduce emissions from urban transport in the absence of additional policies. This underlines the scale of the challenge of decarbonising urban transport in Auckland.
- **Increasing the use of public transport while imposing higher taxes on private vehicles offers one pathway to emission reductions.** The report examines a package of policies that promotes public transport over private vehicles. This package drastically increases the cost of private vehicle ownership while channelling a large subsidy to public transport fares. This policy package targets a modal shift to public transport and reduces aggregate emissions by 40% in 2050, relative to the reference case in which these policies are not implemented. Further, the public transport policy package yields a welfare gain equivalent to 0.9% of net income in 2050. Therefore, incentivising a switch to public transport, while ensuring that public transport is electrified should be a priority.
- **Promoting the use of electric vehicles over conventional and hybrid vehicles offers another path to large reductions in emissions from urban transport.** The report also examines a policy package that promotes a shift to electric vehicles. The considered policies channel substantial subsidies and tax exemptions to electric vehicles while significantly increasing the fixed and operating cost of conventional vehicles. This effectively increases the use of electric vehicles. The report finds that these measures increase the share of households that own an electric vehicle to 13.5% and reduce aggregate emissions by 30% in 2050, relative to the reference case. The associated welfare gain is estimated to be 1.6% of net income in 2050. Reducing emissions by supporting the transition to electric vehicles is particularly effective in New Zealand where the share of renewable energy in the electricity grid is very high.
- **Land use policies that affect the spatial structure of a city can play a substantial role in reducing vehicle kilometres travelled.** A general relaxation of density regulations in Auckland can reduce emissions by an additional 10% if implemented in combination with the policy packages that promote public transport and electric vehicles. This reduction in emissions could potentially be even greater if urban densification is combined with a delay in the development of remote suburban areas.
- **In addition to reducing emissions, policies that increase population density may entail further social benefits by curbing the growth in the cost of housing.** By implementing a set of land use policies that enable widespread densification, the tripling of housing prices in Auckland projected in the period 2018-2050 can be reduced to an increase of 57%. The associated welfare gain of such policies is substantial. The report finds that this gain exceeds 7% of net income in 2050.

- **A faster rate of innovation in the electric vehicle industry will increase the penetration rate of electric vehicles and lower transport sector emissions.** Adopting a more optimistic view of the pace of technological change than the one used in the main results leads to a drastic increase in the share of households that own an electric vehicle by 2050. In turn, a higher share of passenger kilometres travelled using electric vehicles reduces aggregate emissions by 30% between 2018 and 2050. More rapid technological development also enhances the effectiveness of transport policies that support the penetration of these vehicles.

Implementing the policies assessed in the report will require co-ordinated and targeted action at both national and local levels. Reducing emissions from urban transport is most effective when transport and land use policies are integrated. A combination of policies is required to incentivise modal shifts, reduce emissions intensity per kilometre travelled and reduce total distances travelled. Trade-offs between environmental and welfare outcomes should be considered in order to ensure cost-efficient policies. Moreover, it can take time for land use and transport policies to affect the urban structure of a city and the composition of its vehicle fleet. The report highlights the areas in which there is a need for rapid policy action if the targeted reductions are to be achieved.

The policy recommendations included in the report also holds relevance to contexts beyond Auckland, particularly to urban areas characterised by low population density and car dependency. However, the design of these policies should be adapted to the local characteristics of each specific area. To achieve this objective, the report examines the extent to which the results of the analysis change when certain underlying assumptions are modified.

References

C40 (2019), *Transportation and urban planning initiative: Mass Transit*, C40 Cities, https://www.c40.org/networks/mass-transit. [3]

IEA (2018), *CO2 Emissions from Fuel Combustion 2018*. [2]

IPCC (2018), "Summary for Policymakers", in Masson-Delmotte, V. et al. (eds.), *Global warming of 1.5°C. An IPCC Special Report on the impacts of global warming of 1.5°C above pre-industrial levels and related global greenhouse gas emission pathways*, World Meteorological Organization, Geneva. [1]

Chapter 1. The challenges related to decarbonising transport in low-density urban areas

This chapter frames the overall importance of decarbonising transport in low-density urban areas, the responses available to policy makers and their anticipated impact. The challenge is considerable, as cities are currently home to 50% of world's population but are responsible for 60-80% of global CO2 emissions. Urban policy action is imperative, since city populations and global urban land cover will continue growing and technological solutions alone will not suffice to offset that growth. Rapid policy interventions on the areas detailed in the report should therefore be prioritised if the targeted emission reductions are to be achieved.

1.1. Why is urban transport important in tackling climate change?

Urbanisation has been one of the cornerstones of economic expansion in the 20th century. For decades, uninterrupted economic growth has fuelled, and been fuelled by, growth in urban areas and urban populations. Slowly, a series of interrelated challenges have emerged, exerting pressure on the ability of cities to generate prosperity. Climate change is at the forefront of these issues and its impacts on natural systems and human communities are already being felt (IPCC, 2018[1]).

The economic, geographic and demographic prominence of cities makes them central to climate change mitigation. By 2050, about 70% of the world's population is expected to live in urban areas, a figure that could be as high as 85% in OECD countries. Over the same period, global urban land cover is projected to increase five-fold: from approximately 600 000 km^2 in 2011, to 3 million km^2 of land in 2050 (Angel et al., 2011[2]). Given these trends, cities will play an increasingly central role in the effort to reduce greenhouse gas emissions from human activities.

There are critical differences in the consumption patterns that underlie urban and rural lifestyles. People in urban areas have higher incomes, use energy-intensive services for transport, housing and recreational purposes and benefit from the provision of energy-intensive facilities that often do not exist in rural areas. These characteristics make cities particularly relevant for efforts to reduce greenhouse gas emissions. Furthermore, road travel in urban areas often takes place on congested roadways at low average speeds, leading to greater fuel consumption and emissions per kilometre travelled, relative to optimal conditions. As a result, the *per capita* carbon footprint of urban populations is larger than that of rural populations: cities are currently home to 50% of world's population but are responsible for 60-80% of global CO_2 emissions (OECD, 2010[3]). This share is likely to increase as urbanisation continues uninterrupted. Therefore, climate action at the city level is an essential element of policy portfolios to limit the rise in global average temperature.

Decarbonising urban transport is a crucial part of such policy action, as reducing emissions in this sector is particularly challenging. Greenhouse gas emissions from transport make up approximately one third of total urban greenhouse gas emissions in major cities and constitute a significant obstacle in the pursuit of emissions reduction targets (C40, 2019[4]). Transport-related emissions have risen faster than in any other sector over the past three decades. Reducing the emissions generated by the transport sector will require a shift away from fossil fuel powered vehicles and a move towards public transport and electric vehicles. Decarbonising the power generation sector is an important component of strategies that shift transport towards electromobility.

1.2. What policies can be deployed to reduce transport emissions at the urban level?

Policies can reduce emissions from the transport sector through multiple channels:

1. Reducing the emissions intensity per *passenger kilometre* travelled, by encouraging a shift from private vehicles to public transport, biking or walking and by incentivising carpooling or car sharing.
2. Reducing the emissions intensity per *vehicle kilometre* travelled, through measures that encourage shifts from fossil fuel-powered cars to electric vehicles (EVs).

3. Reducing the emissions intensity per *vehicle kilometre* travelled, through incentives to use more energy-efficient vehicles.
4. Reducing the emissions intensity per *vehicle kilometre* travelled with electric vehicles, by investing in less carbon-intensive modes of electricity generation.
5. Reducing the *total number of kilometres* travelled, by encouraging fewer trips, for instance by making trips more expensive or by incentivising teleworking.
6. Reducing the *total number of kilometres* travelled, by shortening trip distances, for instance by incentivising compact urban forms.

The primary focus of the report is on policies that reduce emissions *mainly* through channels 1, 2, 5 and 6. Such policies make use of the following instruments: kilometre taxes on the use of private vehicles; fuel taxes; road pricing; annual circulation fees; public transport subsidies; exemptions of EVs from various pricing mechanisms; purchase subsidies to EVs; non-pecuniary incentives for EV use, such as the right to use bus lanes; building-height restrictions; and private open space regulations.

Most of the above *transport policies* affect the decision to own a vehicle, the choice of vehicle type and the way that vehicle will be utilised. Therefore, they have an impact on the ownership rates, the shares of different vehicle types in the fleet and the overall level of traffic. Transport policies play a key role in determining the average carbon footprint of a passenger and a vehicle kilometre. Furthermore, these instruments affect the *modal split*, i.e. the percentage of trips or kilometres traversed by each mode of transportation.

Policies whose primary aim is to reduce private vehicle ownership could lower emissions through their impact on the size of the vehicle fleet. Such policies increase the generalised cost of owning and operating a private vehicle. For instance, they can increase registration and annual circulation fees, fuel taxes, parking fees and other relevant road use charges. They could also include measures such as transit fare subsidies, which increase the attractiveness of public transport.

Policies whose primary target is a shift in modal split should be part of the overall effort to decarbonise urban transport. Such policies increase the relative cost of private vehicle use *vis-à-vis* other, greener forms of urban mobility, like public transport, but also cycling and walking. This change in relative cost can be achieved either by increasing the generalized cost of car use, for instance through parking fees and road use charges, or by reducing the generalised cost of public transport and soft mobility options. For instance, investments in dedicated bike roads and in infrastructure for pedestrians can be included in the latter category.

Policies that mainly promote EVs are also key, as these vehicles can play a major role in reducing greenhouse gas (hereafter, GHG) emissions generated from urban road transport. This is particularly the case in countries like New Zealand, where the carbon intensity of electricity generation is very low (Transpower, 2018[5]). Provided this, a switch to electric vehicles will entail a drastic reduction in transport-related GHG emissions. However, in order for this transition to occur, the cost of owning and operating an EV must fall steeply relative to a conventional internal combustion engine vehicle (hereafter, ICE vehicle). Convergence to parity between ICE vehicles and EVs through technological development is a slow process, calling for policies that increase the generalised cost of ICE vehicles vis-à-vis EVs. Typically, such policies subsidise the purchase of EVs, grant them preferential treatment with respect to their daily use and exempt them from pricing mechanisms that apply to ICE vehicles.

Land use and urban planning policies have a less obvious but considerable effect on urban transport emissions, particularly in the long run. These policies determine the spatial distribution of economic activity and population density and therefore have an impact on transport demand and long-run travel patterns. If these policies foster sparser residential development and discourage mixed land use, an urban development pattern characterised by larger distances between residences, jobs, shopping and leisure locations is more likely to emerge. In turn, greater sprawl implies greater use of motorised transport and more dependence on private vehicles. This has significant environmental implications, underlining the importance of land use and urban planning tools.

Urban structure has long been known to affect the carbon footprint of a city. The predominance of a low-density residential development pattern, also known as *urban sprawl*, is statistically associated with a steep increase in *per capita* GHG emissions from the transport sector. Cities with a lower average population density are in general more dispersed, as their key points of economic activity (jobs, residences, shopping malls, leisure hubs) lie at larger distances from each other (OECD, 2018[6]). Thus, the number of *per capita* passenger kilometres is generally higher in sprawled urban areas. The same is true for the carbon intensity of the average passenger kilometre in sprawled cities, as these are often highly dependent on car use and highly congested. Due to their low density, these cities are also less likely to offer extensive public transport systems whose services efficiently cover the urban fabric. The literature has explored various other channels through which the negative relationship between density and transport-related energy consumption is formed.

The environmental ramifications of urban development patterns are significant. This holds true because the relationship between density and transport-related energy consumption is highly non-linear: very high fuel consumption is observed in areas of low population density (Newman and Kenworthy, 1989[7]). As population density increases, the corresponding fall in fuel consumption grows progressively smaller. This means that an increase in population density in a low-density area is associated with a larger decrease in fuel consumption, than the same increase in an area of high population density (Newman and Kenworthy, 1989[7]; Mindali, Raveh and Salomon, 2004[8]).

Moreover, urban development patterns are an integral part of successful public transport systems, namely because these systems are more expensive to provide in low-density areas. Thus, policies that increase population density may reduce the subsidies public transport requires (OECD, 2018[6]). As a result, policy reforms targeting a greener modal split are more effective in compact settings, where public transport services and soft mobility infrastructure can be provided at a lower social cost. However, a more compact urban form, in which multi-family dwellings are the predominant type of development, may present certain barriers to the widespread adoption of EVs. This holds true especially if the development pattern is characterised by a lack of private parking spaces, where EVs can be recharged. In that sense, densification policies may be synergistic or antagonistic with respect to other policies intended to decarbonise urban transport. A more comprehensive understanding of these potential interactions is therefore warranted.

Policies that promote a more compact urban form are fundamental in the long-run success of urban transport decarbonisation strategies. Such policies may include the relaxation of building height restrictions and the acceleration of infill development. The former measure allows buildings to be higher, resulting in more residential floor space in the long run. The latter measure reduces private open space, e.g. backyards between buildings or dwellings. Both measures can be spatially differentiated, i.e. they can be applied only in designated areas where densification is environmentally relevant and economically efficient. For example, governments can prioritise densification in areas where land use is mixed, i.e. in areas where residences coexist with jobs, shopping facilities and other key points of economic activity. By increasing housing supply in these areas, policy makers bring a larger part of the population closer to areas of economic activity, thereby shortening average trip length. In turn, the reduction of trip distances could lead to sizeable reductions in vehicle kilometres and thus in greenhouse gas emissions. Similarly, policy makers may choose to postpone densification in remote suburban residential areas that lie far from the key points of economic activity.

Each of the policies examined in the report can reduce emissions through multiple channels. For instance, increasing fuel taxes may trigger higher shares of carpooling and biking or it may cause some car users to switch to public transport, reducing the carbon footprint of each kilometre they travel. Additionally, increased fuel taxes may also generate incentives for people to acquire more fuel-efficient cars, vehicles that do not use conventional fuel, e.g. EVs, or to relocate their residence closer to the end destination of their trips. Therefore, each of the aforementioned policies could have an impact on more behavioural margins than the ones it was initially designed to affect.

Different policies take effect across different time horizons. Typically, the effects of transport policies are quick to manifest, while the effects of land-use policies are slower to materialise. In the short run, changes in driving behaviour, such as adjustments in speed and vehicle route, can have an direct impact on fuel consumption and, consequently, on emissions from urban transport. Policies including road pricing and parking fees may also affect behaviour in the near term and are likely to relocate traffic and reduce its external effects. The various impacts of policies, as they materialise in the short, medium and long term, should be carefully evaluated in order to design socially desirable policies that accelerate the transition to green mobility.

The exact social cost of decarbonising urban transport with the measures described in this chapter is highly context-specific, i.e. it depends on the urban area under examination. For example, promoting public transport in compact urban areas comes at a significantly lower social cost than in sprawled cities characterised by fragmented public transport systems. The greater social cost incurred in sprawled urban areas arises primarily from the fact that populations living in these areas are more likely to depend on private vehicles. Therefore, increasing the pecuniary cost of car use in these areas may cut down tailpipe emissions, but it is also likely to reduce the well-being of those without a viable alternative to car. Promoting public transport through fare subsidies will not necessarily lower the social cost of such reform, as these subsidies have to be financed through taxes. Additionally, fare subsidies have to be of a considerable magnitude in order to induce significant changes in urban mobility patterns. This narrative is possibly much different in a compact urban area, in which the aforementioned policies could thrive much easier. This example illustrates the degree to which the success of transport policies is contingent on existing land use patterns.

Therefore, the various general strategies for decarbonising transport proposed in this report have to be tailored to the exact context of each specific city. The optimal mix of decarbonisation policies in a city depends on its spatial layout, the configuration of its networks and its various land use and transport regulatory mechanisms. Importantly, optimal decarbonisation strategies also depend on the wider socioeconomic background of the area and on key technological parameters that characterise the energy sector. The city case study elaborated in this report carefully controls for the above considerations. It takes into account the various idiosyncratic characteristics and gauges the extent to which these distinctive elements drive the key findings. With this approach, the report provides both overarching policy recommendations, applicable to numerous urban areas around the world, as well as more detailed proposals that apply to the urban area of Auckland, New Zealand.

1.3. Policy context and approach

This report provides an in-depth examination of various decarbonisation strategies for the urban transport of Auckland, the biggest and fastest growing city in New Zealand. Auckland faces a series of structural and demographic challenges common to many cities around the world. These challenges include low population density, which is associated with high costs of public transport provision, and car dependency, which acts as a barrier to reducing the city's future carbon footprint (OECD, 2018[6]). The above characteristics contribute to the share of greenhouse gas emissions generated by road transport in Auckland (37.6%), which is high but comparable to that of other sprawled cities (Xie, 2017[9]; Auckland Transport, 2018[10]). Furthermore, New Zealand has the highest rate of car ownership in the OECD and has a relatively old and inefficient car fleet (OECD, 2017[11]; Ministry for the Environment & Stats NZ, 2019[12]). As a result, emissions from road transport make up 39% of all carbon dioxide emissions, which is significantly higher than in many other developed countries (Ministry for the Environment & Stats NZ, 2019[12]).

Auckland's low population density, high degree of car dependency, and inefficient provision of public transport are closely related to the issue of diminishing *housing affordability* in the city. Between 1990 and 2017, real house prices in Auckland rose by 300% (The Economist, 2019[13]). Growth in house prices has been more rapid than growth in wages: between 2002 and 2014 the median house price in Auckland increased by 159%, while the median income increased by just 46% (Tuatagaloa, 2017[14]). Rapid population growth and stringent land-use regulations are the primary drivers of rising housing prices. While some land-use regulations in Auckland are motivated by the local importance of volcanic view shafts and the need for stormwater disposal, they have prevented housing supply from meeting the growing demand (New Zealand Social Investment Agency, 2017[15]). As such, the regulatory mechanisms that generate the conditions for car dependency also contribute to higher housing prices. This means that policy initiatives regarding land-use regulation could both reduce greenhouse gas emissions from mobile sources and address the issue of housing affordability.

The study assesses a series of policies, presented in detail in the previous section, which can be grouped into three broad categories. The first category contains policies set to induce a massive switch from private vehicles to public transport, essentially through pricing and subsidy instruments designed to increase the cost of the former relative to the latter. Through a similar set of measures, a second category attempts to generate a massive switch from ICE vehicles to EVs. Finally, the third category includes instruments that aim to develop a compact urban form in the long run, in which trip distances will be smaller and daily travel much less energy demanding.

The report assesses these policies from various viewpoints. First, it reports the environmental impact of each policy by calculating the associated change in greenhouse gas emissions and by converting that change into a monetised measure of social welfare. Second, it computes the social welfare benefit and cost of the aforementioned policies. In particular, the study monetises the impacts from changes in congestion, housing prices and household budgets. Finally, the study gauges the fiscal effect of each proposed policy by calculating its impact on the revenue generated by key existing taxes. For instance, the analysis contains calculations of the effect of a change in the kilometre tax on the revenue generated by fuel taxes. Through this approach, the report estimates the social value of the fiscal surpluses or deficits a policy induces.

The analysis is carried out with the use of the Multi-Objective Local Environmental Simulator (MOLES), an urban Computable General Equilibrium (u-CGE) model constructed by the OECD in order to examine the environmental effectiveness and economic efficiency of urban policies targeting land use and transport. The report presents a specific version of MOLES that has been tailored to account for the particular characteristics of Auckland. The urban area's spatial layout, the physical configuration of its transport networks, the mobility patterns of its population and the prevailing traffic conditions are some of the key elements that the model either uses as input or is calibrated to reproduce.

1.4. Key questions, findings and the contribution of the report

The report seeks to provide answers to three overarching questions:

- Will technological change in the electric vehicle industry lead to significant reductions in urban tailpipe emissions?
- What is the role of transport and land use policies in reducing urban greenhouse gas emissions?
- Are these policies welfare improving, once their wider impact on the economy and society is taken into account?

The study thoroughly investigates the first question, which is key since a switch to electromobility could significantly reduce transport sector emissions. That is, the analysis goes beyond providing an answer for the case of New Zealand, where the carbon intensity of a kilometre driven by an EV is particularly low. It also attempts to provide insights from a global perspective, in which the electricity used to power EVs is on average much more carbon intensive.

With respect to the second question, the report examines the degree to which policies targeting land use and transport are effective means of reducing greenhouse gas emissions. In line with that, the analysis offers several insights on the behaviour changes that may occur with the implementation of these policies. The report explains how each policy works and why some of the considered policies may fail to deliver the results they were hoped to. The underlying modelling approach factors in the interaction between national policies, such as taxes on gasoline and electricity, and local policies, such as parking fees and urban road pricing. Furthermore, it examines the degree to which these findings depend on the most important working assumptions through an extensive sensitivity analysis, which facilitates comparison with other studies.

The third question regards the aggregate social costs and benefits of the examined land use and transport policies. While a considerable share of this report's focus lies on the environmental effectiveness of various policies, their socioeconomic impacts – whether positive or negative – can be substantial. This is primarily because the policies considered in the study affect private budgets, as well as land and housing prices, and thus alter housing affordability and the daily cost of living. The report controls for this aspect by assessing each policy's economic efficiency, i.e. the associated social cost stemming from these wider impacts. Furthermore, many of the investigated policy instruments are essentially taxes whose adjustment alters the base of other important taxes. For instance, an adjustment of the flat kilometre tax – a policy the report places emphasis on due to its widespread use in New Zealand – causes a change in the level of car use and thus affects the revenue of the fuel tax. In this way, the analysis explicitly accounts for the social costs stemming from the erosion of tax bases. The above impacts are then incorporated into detailed cost-benefit calculations, resulting in the construction of a single welfare measure. That measure captures the environmental effectiveness, economic efficiency and fiscal impact of each policy. Given that the measure permits the direct comparison of policies whose various impacts differ widely, it is highly relevant as a tool for policy development.

The report highlights the overall importance of targeted mitigation policies as a complement to technological progress and innovation. It finds that substantial policy interventions are required to reduce total emissions from urban transport. Although technological developments will likely decrease urban transport emissions *per capita*, they will offset only a part of the expected rise in total emissions from urban transport. Under the reference scenario, in which no substantial policy change occurs, total emissions from road transport will continue increasing. In 2050, technological progress – as it is projected to occur in the reference scenario of the report – will have lowered *per capita* emissions by only 40% relative to 2018. Therefore, the projections show that technological evolution *per se* will be far from sufficient to ensure carbon neutrality by 2050.

The results indicate that promoting the use of public transport offers one major pathway to emission reductions. Measures aiming to increase the private cost of vehicle ownership and to decrease the private cost of public transport use could yield significant reductions in aggregate emissions. Policies that promote public transport can reduce *per capita* emissions from urban transport by 25% relative to their levels in 2018. The latter reduction comes on top of the 40% reduction stemming from expected technical progress. The analysis shows that in order for policies promoting public transport to be successful from a social viewpoint, they will have to combine a set of substantial increases in the kilometre cost of car use with sizeable public transport fare subsidies. A successful combination of these policy elements could generate welfare gains that account for 1% of income.

One of the most striking findings of the report is that the pecuniary-based public transport policies such as fare subsidies or private vehicle road pricing are unlikely to induce a massive shift away from private car ownership, especially in urban areas like Auckland. Many cities around the world remain heavily car-dependent, as the population density in a large share of their footprint is low, travel distances within them are long and public transport services are inefficient or unreliable. Dependency on private vehicles limits the degree to which policies promoting public transport can successfully increase public transport use in these areas. This limitation will subside only after the key characteristics of their public transport systems, such as spatial coverage, connectivity, comfort and reliability, improve substantially.

The degree to which a shift to public transport can ensure a substantial reduction in greenhouse gas emissions depends on the composition of the fleet of public transport vehicles. The extent to which public transport is electrified is important, as public transport in many cities around the world remains heavily reliant on diesel-powered buses. The carbon intensity of the electricity grid is also important, as a switch to public electromobility entails a larger reduction in greenhouse gas emissions when the consumed electricity has a lower carbon footprint.

Promoting the use of electric vehicles may offer another path to considerable reductions in emissions from urban transport. The findings show that the associated policies increase the ownership rate and use of electric vehicles and reduce the respective figures for ICE vehicles, leading to a 20% reduction in the *per capita* greenhouse gas emissions from urban transport.

The report also highlights the extent to which an accelerated adoption of EVs will significantly reduce greenhouse gas emissions, as this reduction depends on the carbon intensity of the electricity-generating sector. For instance, the mitigation potential of EV adoption can be drastic in New Zealand, where the share of renewable energy in the electricity grid is very high. However, that is not necessarily the case in other parts of the world, where the carbon intensity of electricity generation is higher. That conclusion is supported by the fact that the amount of CO_2 emitted to produce one kilowatt-hour of electricity in New Zealand is lower than the OECD average by a factor of four (IEA, 2017[16]). In countries with a lower share of energy generated from renewable sources, emissions from electricity generation could undermine the potential of policies promoting electromobility to reduce greenhouse gas emissions. Therefore, policies supporting electric vehicles should be accompanied by a decarbonisation of the electricity generation sector.

One of the study's most notable findings is that land-use policies have substantial long run potential to reduce urban transport emissions. The analysis reveals that a general relaxation of density regulations, which gives rise to a more compact urban form, may act as an effective complement to policies that promote public transport. When the latter policies are present, densification policies eliminate a further 5% of total emissions from urban transport. This figure, which is derived within the context of Auckland and its expected development to 2050, can be much higher if densification is combined with restrictions on the development of remote suburban areas.

Apart from their environmental impact, the report highlights the wider social benefits that reforms in land use regulations may bring. For instance, the results indicate that widespread densification, which implies an increase in housing supply, slows the growth in the cost of housing. The associated welfare gain of such a policy is substantial, as the report finds that it exceeds 7% of net income in Auckland in 2050. Cities with comparable characteristics are likely to be able to achieve similar outcomes.

The policies examined in the report do not suffice to eliminate greenhouse gas emissions from urban transport. That is, the expected technological growth and the various land-use and transport policies eliminate up to 70% of the *per capita* emissions by 2050. Eliminating the remaining 30% of emissions requires substantial investments in public transport infrastructure, as well as in research and development (R&D) that has a potential to accelerate innovation in key areas relevant to the transport sector. Speeding up technical progress in the electric vehicle industry, solving energy storage challenges and developing cheaper batteries will accelerate the penetration rate of electric vehicles.

This report outlines pathways for cutting greenhouse gas emissions from urban transport in Auckland and in other areas with similar characteristics. Looking ahead to 2050, policy action to reduce emissions from the transport sector is critical for achieving the targets set under the Paris Agreement and the SDGs. Land use and transport policies are slow to take effect on the urban structure of a city and the composition of its vehicle fleet. The report highlights the areas in which there is a need for rapid policy action if the targeted reductions are to be achieved.

1.5. Navigation through the report

The report is developed in two parts. The first part, which spans Chapters 2 to 4, lays out the methodological context of the analysis. It provides a detailed description of the various scenarios, data sources, the way they were processed and their role in the study. It also describes, in a non-technical manner, the model used in the policy simulations and its ability to reflect the empirical regularities of Auckland and New Zealand. The second part, which spans Chapters 5 and 6, presents the findings of the analysis and their sensitivity to the working assumptions made *a priori*. It therefore provides a series of policy insights that apply to Auckland and to other urban areas facing similar challenges.

Chapter 2 presents the baseline scenario, as well as the various counterfactual scenarios examined in the study. The former scenario is also referred to as the reference scenario, since it constitutes the reference case in which all currently implemented policies are kept fixed and all currently announced policies for the period from 2019 to 2050 materialise. In contrast, the chapter presents various counterfactual scenarios that introduce new land use and transport policies in the same period.

Chapter 3 provides a non-technical description of MOLES, an urban CGE model OECD developed to evaluate the environmental and economic impact of land use and transport policies. The chapter presents a version of MOLES that is tailored to incorporate a number of important characteristics of Auckland's urban area in the analysis. It details how the behaviour of households and real-estate developers is modelled and elaborates on the way housing and land markets function in the model. It also describes how the various outcomes of the modelling exercise, which include transport, emission, welfare, housing and fiscal indicators, are calculated.

Chapter 4 provides a navigation of the various data sources and model calibration. The first part of the chapter describes and visualizes how land use and travel survey data are combined to create a stylised representation of Auckland's spatial layout. The chapter elaborates on the use of other data sources, such as traffic, census and vehicle fleet data. exhibits the fit of the model to the empirical regularities of Auckland and New Zealand. The second part of the chapter provides details on the various stylised facts MOLES simulations yield in the benchmark year of the study, i.e. 2018. These include the way households spend their income and allocate their time, as well as their travel behaviour and its sensitivity to changes in price and income.

Chapter 5 exhibits the key findings of the report, i.e. the results from the evaluation of reference and counterfactual scenarios. These include the environmental, housing, fiscal and welfare implications of the various scenarios in which different transport and land use policies are implemented. The results also highlight the impacts of policy inaction, which is evaluated with the use of the reference scenario. The environmental and economic impact of the various interventions is shown to be particularly diverse: the various policies may yield very different welfare effects, whose magnitude depends on the time frame in which these policies are implemented. Therefore, the analysis does not only focus on highlighting the policies that curb greenhouse gas emissions and increase welfare, but also on identifying the optimal timeline for implementing these policies.

Chapter 6 explores the degree to which the key policy recommendations of the study are applicable beyond the case of Auckland. To this end, it demonstrates the effect of changing several key assumptions on the projected reductions in greenhouse gas emissions. Moreover, the chapter offers an extensive sensitivity analysis with respect to various model parameters. This analysis identifies the factors and parameters that have an important impact on the key conclusions of the report. It also facilitates the adjustment of key policy recommendations to other contexts, i.e. in settings where these factors and parameters may differ substantially from Auckland. Finally, the chapter enumerates a series of methodological limitations of the analysis and the impact they have on the key conclusions.

References

Angel, S. et al. (2011), *Making Room for a Planet of Cities*, Lincoln Institute of Land Policy, http://www.lincolninst.edu/sites/default/files/pubfiles/ making-room-for-a-planet-of-cities-full_0.pdf. [2]

Auckland Transport (2018), *Auckland's Low Emission Bus Roadmap.* [10]

C40 (2019), *Transportation and urban planning initiative: Mass Transit*, C40 Cities, https://www.c40.org/networks/mass-transit. [4]

IEA (2017), *Energy Policies of IEA Countries - New Zealand*, International Energy Agency, http://www.iea.org/t&c/. [16]

IPCC (2018), "Summary for Policymakers", in Masson-Delmotte, V. et al. (eds.), *Global warming of 1.5°C. An IPCC Special Report on the impacts of global warming of 1.5°C above pre-industrial levels and related global greenhouse gas emission pathways*, World Meteorological Organization, Geneva. [1]

Mindali, O., A. Raveh and I. Salomon (2004), "Urban density and energy consumption: A new look at old statistics", *Transportation Research Part A: Policy and Practice*, http://dx.doi.org/10.1016/j.tra.2003.10.004. [8]

Ministry for the Environment & Stats NZ (2019), *New Zealand's Environmental Reporting Series: Environment Aotearoa 2019.*, Ministry for the Environment and Stats NZ, http://www.mfe.govt.nz. [12]

New Zealand Social Investment Agency (2017), *Quantifying the impact of land use regulation: Evidence from New Zealand*, https://thehub.sia.govt.nz/assets/documents/Impact_land_use_summary_110717.pdf. [15]

Newman, P. and J. Kenworthy (1989), "Gasoline consumption and cities: A comparison of U.S. cities with a global survey", *Journal of the American Planning Association*, http://dx.doi.org/10.1080/01944368908975398. [7]

OECD (2018), *Rethinking Urban Sprawl*, OECD Publishing. [6]

OECD (2017), *OECD Environmental Performance Reviews: Estonia 2017*, OECD Environmental Performance Reviews, OECD Publishing, Paris, https://dx.doi.org/10.1787/9789264268241-en. [11]

OECD (2010), *Cities and Climate Change*, OECD Publishing, Paris, http://dx.doi.org/10.1787/9789264091375-en. [3]

The Economist (2019), *Global cities house-price index.* [13]

Transpower (2018), *Te Mauri Hiko - Energy Futures*, https://www.transpower.co.nz/sites/default/files/publications/resources/TP Energy Futures - Te Mauri Hiko 21 May%2718 - web.pdf. [5]

Tuatagaloa, P. (2017), *Affordability of Housing in Auckland-Who Will Teach Our Children? A Discussion Paper*. [14]

Xie, S. (2017), *Auckland's Greenhouse Gas Inventory to 2015*, Auckland Council. [9]

Part I.

Analytical framework

Chapter 2. Building scenarios for the long-run evolution of urban areas

This chapter presents the reference scenario, as well as the various counterfactual scenarios examined in the study. The first section details the projected evolution of exogenous factors such as population and income, which impact the results. The second section describes the reference scenario, in which all currently implemented policies are kept fixed and all announced policies materialise. The third section elaborates on the various counterfactual scenarios, which introduce new land use and transport policies in the period from 2019 to 2050.

A *scenario* is composed of two distinct elements. The first element is a set of hypotheses about the variables that evolve over time and play an important role in determining the outcomes of the modelling exercise, but are not affected by these outcomes. Such key variables, which are referred to as *exogenous*, include the various components of vehicles' user costs, the urban population and the pre-tax prices of vehicles, fuel and electricity. The complete list of exogenous variables and their associated definitions is presented in Table 2.1.

Table 2.1. Exogenous variables

Variables that affect the model's outcomes but are not affected by them.

Variable	Explanation
Population	The total number of individuals residing in the city in a given year
Pre-tax vehicle price	The price of a representative vehicle in a given year, net of excise and value-added taxes
Pre-tax fuel & electricity price	The average per litre price of fuel and per kWh price of electricity in a given year, net of excise and ad-valorem taxes.
Fuel economy	The fuel consumption (lt/km) of a representative internal combustion engine (ICE) vehicle[a] in a given year.
Electricity consumption	The electricity consumption (kWh/km) of a representative electric vehicle (EV) in a given year.

Note: [a]This vehicle is representative of gasoline, diesel and hybrid cars.

The second set of inputs in a scenario consists of assumptions about the state of *policy instruments* that impact the outcomes of the modelling exercise. Important variables include: (i) policies determining average emissions per vehicle kilometre, such as the fiscal treatment of conventional and electric vehicles; (ii) policy instruments affecting the relative attractiveness of public transport alternatives (*vis-à-vis* that of privately owned vehicles), such as road pricing, on-street parking fees and public transport subsidies; and (iii) land use policy instruments that determine the driving distances and the degree of car dependency in the long run, such as density regulations.

The study generates outcomes that depend on the values assumed for the exogenous variables and policy instruments. These outcomes, which are referred to as *endogenous variables*, include, but are not limited to, the car ownership rate, the adoption rate of electric vehicles and the population density. Other key outcomes include the endogenous prices of land and housing, which vary across residential zones. As they are endogenous, the above outcomes cannot be used as inputs in the construction of scenarios. Instead, these outcomes are used to qualitatively and quantitatively evaluate the results of the modelling exercise. For instance, the adoption rate of electric vehicles in a given urban area is the outcome of certain policies, relevant prices and unique characteristics of the area. Thus, no valid scenarios can be built by assuming an *ex-ante* EV adoption rate. Rather, economic and environmental implications are calculated based on the EV adoption rate resulting from the exogenous and policy instrument variables defined under a given scenario.

The economic and environmental outcomes under different policy scenarios are evaluated against a single reference scenario. The reference scenario reflects a continuation of current land-use and transport policies into future years. It therefore constitutes a business-as-usual benchmark, against which other *counterfactual policy options* can be evaluated. Examples of counterfactual policies are tax and fee exemptions for electric vehicles or policies that lower the pecuniary cost of public transport relative to the benchmark level used in the reference scenario.

This chapter is organised in three sections. The first presents the evolution of the set of assumptions common to all scenarios. The second lays out the components of the reference scenario, in which all currently-implemented policies are kept fixed. The third describes the counterfactual policy packages, which introduce new policies to be evaluated.

2.1. The root: common assumptions across all scenarios

The evolution of the exogenous variables presented in Table 2.1 is common across all scenarios. The model simulation particularly depends on two of these variables. These are the population growth rate and the speed at which the key attributes of electric vehicles, such as their battery price, lifetime and their driving range, improve over time.

The rate of urban population growth is a key determinant of model outcomes because it affects the aggregate demand for transport. A larger population translates to more trips of all types. Furthermore, population growth may also imply an increase in the *per capita* demand for transport, especially in monocentric urban settings where the points of interest such as jobs, shopping malls and other services are concentrated within a single central business district (CBD). In such cases, population growth tends to increase the distances between residential areas and the aforementioned points. Finally, an increase in population is likely to generate more traffic congestion and reduce driving speeds, which may increase gasoline consumption and therefore the amount of emissions per kilometre driven.

The evolution of the various attributes of EVs are also an important determinant of model outcomes insofar as they influence the adoption rate of these vehicles. A higher adoption rate of EVs results in a lower carbon footprint per kilometre driven by an average vehicle. The pecuniary attributes of EVs include their private cost components, such as the cost of battery depreciation and electricity consumption per kilometre. The non-pecuniary attributes of EVs include speed, which is similar to that of conventional vehicles, and *driving range*, i.e. the maximum distance that can be driven before the battery has to be recharged. The driving range determines the degree to which the vehicle could be utilised without the limitations imposed by the need for frequent recharging. A limited driving range is more restrictive when the spatial density of EV recharging stations is low.

The values for population growth are obtained as weighted averages of plausible boundary values. The upper bound annual population growth is set at 2.2%, a number that is based on the recent rate of population growth in Auckland (Auckland Council, 2018[1]). That rate implies a doubling of the population in the 32-year time horizon of the study (2018-2050). On the other hand, the lower bound annual population growth rate is 1.3% and constitutes a continuation of the long-run trends in the population growth of the city. That rate implies a population increase of approximately 50% in the time range of the study. The reference scenario weights these values equally, implying an annual population growth rate of 1.75%.

In line with the use of boundary values in population growth, the analysis uses a weighted average of an upper and a lower bound in the evolution of the relevant EV attributes. These bounds capture the uncertainty that characterises the rate of technological change in the electric vehicle industry. In the upper bound, i.e. the optimistic case, the average battery depreciation cost per kilometre falls from NZD 0.048 in 2018, to NZD 0.020 in 2030 and to NZD 0.016 in 2050. Simultaneously, the benchmark driving range of 200 kilometres in 2018 increases to 380 kilometres in 2030 and to 500 kilometres in 2050 (Laffont and Peirano, 2013[2]; Chediak, 2017[3]). The upper bound hence represents a continuation of the rapid decline in battery costs observed during in recent years (Nykvist and Nilsson, 2015[4]).

In the lower bound, i.e. the pessimistic case, technological progress reaches a plateau and then slows down. Due to that deceleration, the value of battery depreciation cost per kilometre falls only slightly, to NZD 0.043 in 2030 and NZD 0.039 in 2050. Battery driving range reaches 235 kilometres in 2030 and 250 kilometres in 2050. Reaching a technological plateau before the interim time point of the study (2030) implies that the cost of battery depreciation per kilometre remains at levels that may be high enough to prevent parity with ICE vehicles (Laffont and Peirano, 2013[2]).

The reference values are selected using weighted averages of the upper and lower bound values. The upper bound value is weighted at 66% and the lower bound is weighted at 34%. This reflects the tendency of historic EV cost projections to underestimate future progress in the industry (Laffont and Peirano, 2013[2]). The lower and upper bound values for population growth and technological change in the EV industry are summarised in Table 2.2.

Table 2.2. Upper and lower bound and weighted values for population growth in Auckland and technological change in EV industry

	2018 Benchmark	Upper bound		Lower bound		Weighted value	
		2030	2050	2030	2050	2030	2050
Population in Auckland	1,300,000	1,690,000	2,600,000	1,518,400	1,965,600	1,604,200	2,282,800
Battery depreciation cost (NZD/km)	0.048 [a]	0.02	0.016	0.043	0.039	0.028	0.024
Driving range (km)	200	380	500	235	250	331	415

Note: [a] This number is calculated by assuming that the battery price is equal to its capacity, expressed in kWh, times the price per unit of battery capacity (expressed in NZD/kWh). The EV lifetime is set to 200 000 kilometres, which is derived by assuming a total number of charges (1000) and a driving range of 200 km.

All scenarios examined in the study contain a series of common assumptions. These common assumptions are hereafter referred to as the "*root*" of all scenarios.

In all scenarios, *public open spaces* of an urban area remain intact throughout the considered period. These spaces include open recreational facilities, parks and conservation areas. The same holds for areas that host: industries, retailers and office spaces; infrastructure such as roads and highways; educational and health facilities; as well as areas that serve special purposes (e.g. cemeteries, defence areas).

Furthermore, key *individual preference parameters* remain fixed. For instance, strong preferences for low-density development at year 2018 are assumed to persist until the terminal period, in 2050.[1] However, the model allows housing consumption to adjust upwards as income grows. That adjustment is larger in the case of low-density housing types, reflecting the general preference for low-density development. A similar logic holds for preferences for leisure time.

Unlike preferences, which are time-invariant, other unobserved factors that evolve over time can play an important role in the choice of vehicle type. Such factors may include habits, beliefs, as well as practical and informational constraints that contribute to the current low penetration rate of EVs. One example of such a constraint is the status quo bias, which may stem from, for example, a lack of information of the current operational costs and attributes of EVs or an unwillingness to switch to a new product that has a different charging time and thus implies changing transport habits. The study assumes that the strength of such unobserved factors subsides over time. As shown in detail in Chapter 5, the asymmetry of these factors between ICE vehicles and EVs subsides slowly but steadily over time. All else equal, the 55% of the unobserved advantages ICE vehicles possess over EVs subsides is eliminated by 2050.

Figure 2.1. Projected evolution of conventional vehicle fuel economy, 2018-2050

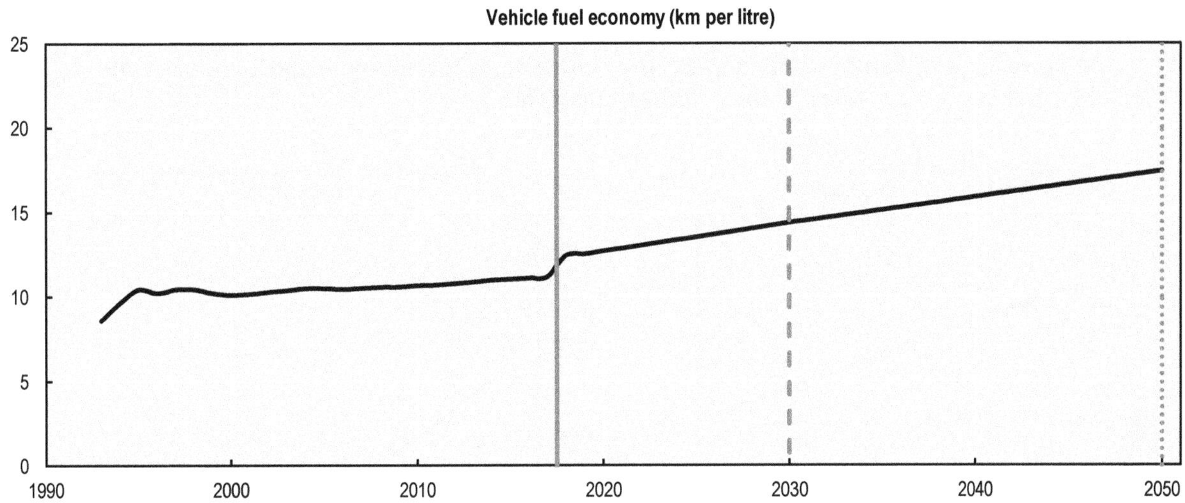

Source: (EPA, 2018[5]; New Zealand Transport Agency, 2018[6]).

The *fuel economy* of conventional vehicles in Auckland, a key factor in the choice of vehicle type, is predicted to increase, from the observed average of 11.2 km per litre of gasoline in 2018, to 14.4 km per litre in 2030 and 17.4 km per litre in 2050.[2] The projection covers both conventional (gasoline and diesel) and hybrid cars. It is based on a clear trend observed in the Auckland vehicle fleet between the years 2000 and 2018. The projection is constructed using separate trends in a series of vehicle attributes, such as body weight, engine size and body type. These factors are known to affect fuel consumption (EPA, 2018[5]; New Zealand Transport Agency, 2018[6]). Subsequently, these trends were extrapolated to the study period, using techniques that are described further in Chapter 4.

The fuel economy projections for conventional vehicles are used to calculate the fuel consumption and, by extension, CO_2e emissions per kilometre. The latter is computed by multiplying the CO_2e content of a litre of gasoline with the fuel economy (litres/km). That multiplication produces the CO_2e emission per kilometre travelled, a value that falls over time as fuel economy improves. From a baseline value of 0.211 kgCO_2e per km in 2017, it declines to 0.160 kgCO_2e per km in 2030 and to 0.132 kgCO_2e per km in 2050. This constitutes a projected 37% decline in emissions per kilometre between 2018 and 2050, as displayed in Figure 2.3.

The projections for the changes to the CO_2e emissions per kilometre made in this study can be compared to projections made by the New Zealand Ministry of Transport (NZ MoT) in the Transport Outlook (New Zealand Ministry of Transport, 2017[7]). In the conservative "Base Case" the NZ MoT Transport Outlook projects a 22% decline in the CO_2e emissions per kilometre of gasoline (petrol) vehicles for the period 2014/15-2039/40. There are two primary reasons why the carbon intensity of gasoline vehicles is projected to fall more in this study than in the Transport Outlook: first, the study makes projections to 2050 whereas the Transport Outlook projects changed to 2040. Extending the time period implies greater improvements in fuel economy. Second, the projection in this study covers both conventional vehicles and hybrid vehicles whereas the Transport Outlook projection covers only gasoline-powered vehicles. Hybrid vehicles are, on average, significantly more fuel-efficient than gasoline vehicles and are expected to increase as a share of the fleet. Their inclusion thus increases the expected improvements in fuel efficiency. The implications of the fuel economy projection of conventional vehicles for the results is fully explored in Chapter 6.

Figure 2.2. Projected evolution of electric vehicle fuel efficiency and emission factor of electricity grid

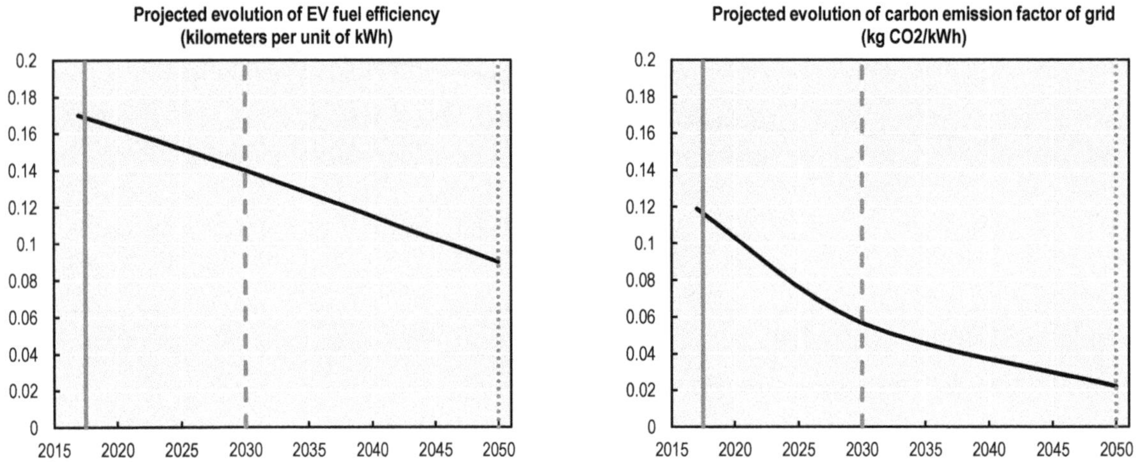

Note: Left panel: projected evolution in electric vehicle fuel efficiency to 2050; right panel: projected evolution in emission factor of electricity grid to 2050.
Source: (Transpower, 2018[8]; IEA, 2017[9]).

The energy efficiency of electric vehicles is projected using a linear extrapolation of the evolution of the energy consumption (kWh/km) of Nissan Leaf, the most popular EV model in New Zealand (New Zealand Transport Agency, 2018[6]; EVDB, 2019[10]). Over time, technological improvements will cause the electricity consumption per kilometre driven to fall. The underlying greenhouse gas emissions of EVs (CO_2e/km) depend on their energy efficiency (kWh/km), as well as on the amount of carbon used in the generation of each energy unit (CO_2e/kWh). Emissions per kilometre fall over time as the electricity required to drive one kilometre falls and the share of renewables in the New Zealand Electricity grid increases (Transpower, 2018[8]; IEA, 2017[9]). These projections are presented in Figure 2.2: the electricity consumption per kilometre falls, from 0.17 kWh per km in 2017 to 0.14 kWh per km in 2030 and to 0.09 kWh per km in 2050. Moreover, the emission factor of the grid falls from 0.119 kgCO_2e per kWh in 2017, to 0.057 kgCO_2e per kWh in 2030 and to 0.022 kgCO_2e per kWh in 2050. This translates to a fall in the emissions per kilometre over time, a change that is shown in Figure 2.3: from a baseline of 0.020 kgCO_2e per km driven for an electric vehicle in 2017 to 0.008 kgCO_2e per km in 2030 and to 0.002 kgCO_2e per km in 2050.

Figure 2.3. Emissions per kilometre of ICE and electric vehicles

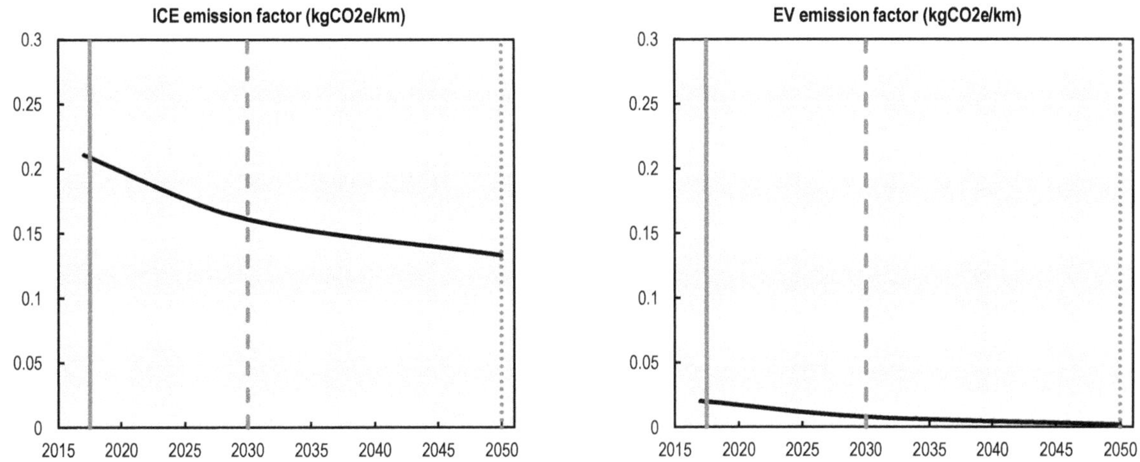

Note: Left panel: projected evolution of per kilometre emissions of ICE vehicles to 2050; right panel: projected evolution of per kilometre emissions of electric vehicles to 2050.
Source: Authors' calculations.

Public transport is projected to become fully electric by 2050, in alignment with the roadmap developed by Auckland Transport (Auckland Transport, 2018[11]). From 2025, Auckland Transport will only procure buses with zero tailpipe emissions and by 2040, the fleet is expected to be fully electric. In line with this procurement plan, the share of electric buses is projected to increase from 0% in 2018 to 25% in 2030 and 100% in 2050. The fuel efficiency of electric buses is projected to improve at the same rate as the one projected for electric passenger vehicles: from the benchmark value of 1.07 kWh per km in 2018, to 0.88 kWh per km in 2030 and to 0.57 kWh in 2050.

The carbon intensity of electric bus travel per passenger-kilometre is calculated by taking the product of three elements: the occupancy rate of buses, their fuel efficiency and the carbon intensity per kWh.[3] The average occupancy rate per kilometre is estimated at an average of 7 passengers in a 35 passenger capacity bus.[4] The occupancy rate is exogenous and is kept fixed across the study period.[5] For example, under a policy scenario promoting public transport the occupancy rate of buses is likely to increase, leading to a fall in the CO_2 emissions per kilometre. However, the potential error introduced will likely be insignificant in assessing total emissions in 2050, as electric buses will consume electricity from an almost clean grid. The study makes an assumption about the evolution of real income of a representative individual. All scenarios assume that this income will continue growing in line with the rates observed during the last three decades.

To extrapolate income growth, the study uses the historical evolution of the *per capita* disposable income in New Zealand, which in Figure 2.4 is expressed as a percentage deviation from its 2017 level. The linear trend, derived for the period 1990-2017, is used to generate positive deviations from the same base year throughout the study period. This implies a real disposable income that in 2030 is roughly 20% higher than that of 2017 and 54% higher in 2050.

Figure 2.4. Percentage deviation of disposable income per capita from its 2017 level.

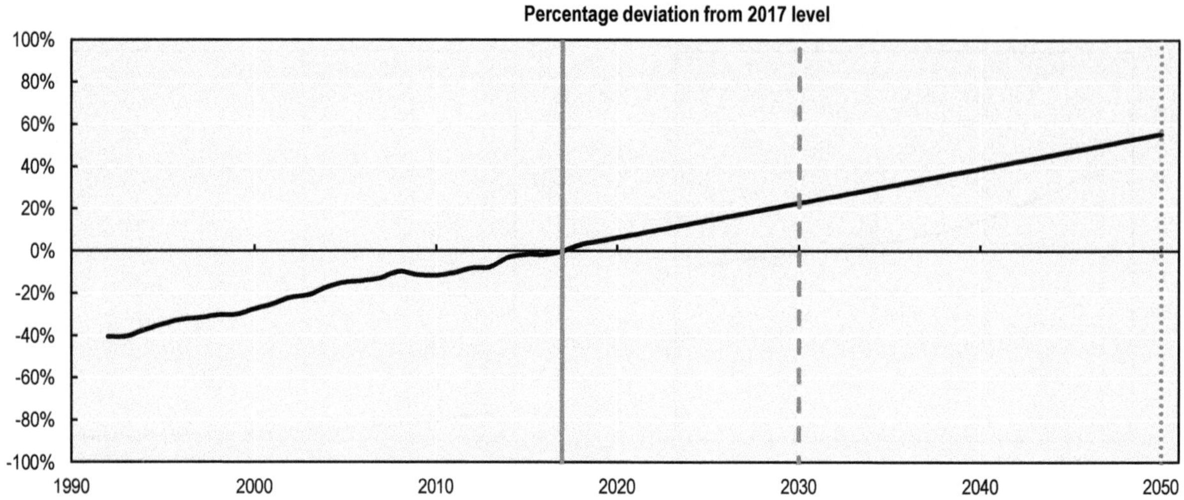

Source: (Statistics New Zealand, 2017[12])

A similar approach is taken to extrapolate electricity prices from the period of observation (2005-2018) to the study period (2018-2050). Real pre-tax residential electricity prices display a clear upward trend between 1980 and 2013, but stabilise in the period 2013-2018 (IEA, 2018[13]). The projected path, shown in the upper panel of Figure 2.5, shows pre-tax electricity prices increasing over time at a pace that gradually slows. This reflects potential technological improvements in power generation and efficiency gains in the use of electricity amid continued demand growth.

Figure 2.5. Projections of real pre-tax residential electricity prices and real pre-tax gasoline prices (1980-2050).

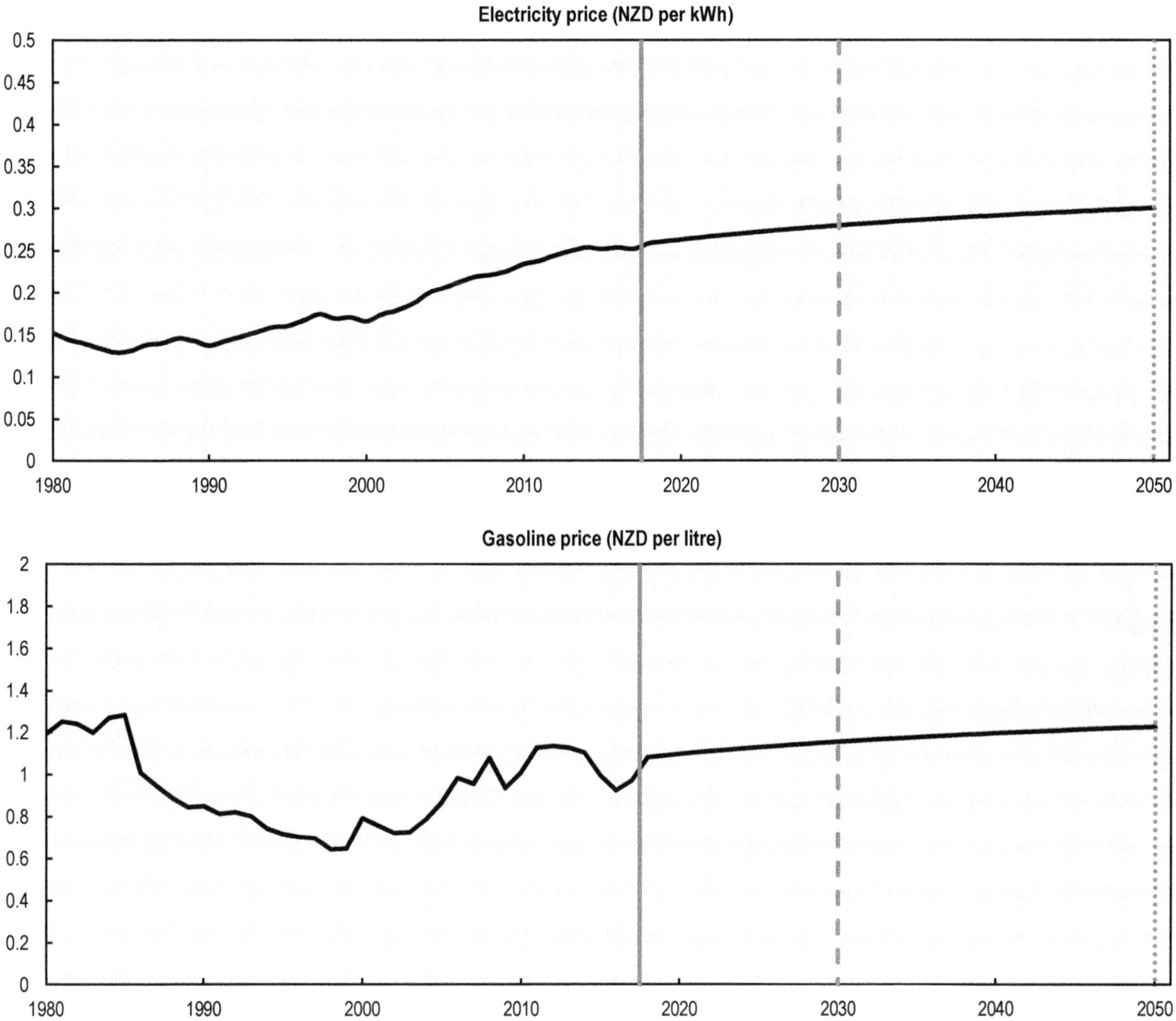

Note: Upper panel: the real pre-tax residential electricity prices. Lower panel: the real pre-tax gasoline prices. 1980-2018 data are used to make projections to 2050.
Sources: (IEA, 2018[14]; IEA, 2018[13]).

The common set of assumptions used in all scenarios is summarised in Table 2.3.[6]

Table 2.3. Root: the common set of assumptions of all scenarios

Element	Assumptions
Household preferences	Preferences remain fixed throughout the entire study period, i.e. from 2018 to 2050.
Income	Compared to 2018, real disposable income is 20% higher in 2030 and 54% higher in 2050.
Pre-tax electricity prices	Compared to 2018, projected pre-tax real electricity prices grow to NZD0.268/kWh in 2030 and NZD0.307/kWh in 2050.[a]
Pre-tax gasoline prices	Compared to 2018, expected real pre-tax gasoline prices increase to NZD 1.07/litre in 2030 and NZD1.17/litre in 2050.[b]
Fuel consumption of conventional vehicles	Fuel economy continues improving. From 11.2 kilometres per litre in 2017, it increases to 14.4 km per litre in 2030 and 17.4 km per litre in 2050.[c]
Emission factor of conventional vehicles	Emissions per km fall over time as the fuel economy of vehicles improves. From 0.211 kgCO_2e per km in 2017, they decrease to 0.160 kgCO_2e per km in 2030 and to 0.132 kgCO_2e per km in 2050.
Electricity consumption of electric vehicles	Technological improvements cause electricity consumption per kilometre to fall throughout the study horizon. From 0.17 kWh per kilometre in 2017, it falls to 0.14 kWh per kilometre in 2030 and to 0.09 kWh per kilometre in 2050.
Emission factor of electricity grid	The rising share of renewables in the New Zealand electricity grid causes the carbon content per kWh to fall. The emission factor of the grid is expected to fall from 0.119 kgCO_2e per kWh in 2017, to 0.057 kgCO_2e per kWh in 2030, to 0.022 kgCO_2e per kWh in 2050
Emission factor of electric vehicles	Emissions per km fall over time as the electricity consumption per kilometre falls and the share of renewables in the New Zealand Electricity grid increases. From 0.020 kgCO_2e per km in 2017, emissions fall to 0.008 kgCO_2e per km in 2030 and to 0.002 kgCO_2e per km in 2050.
Existing public open spaces and facilities	Remain intact throughout the entire study period.
Vehicle bans	Do not apply at any point in time.
Infrastructure	Public transport accessibility increases in selected areas; networks expand proportionately to newly developed areas.
Density of electric vehicle charging stations	Density of charging stations estimated to be 0.03 stations per km^2 of urban fabric in 2018, increasing to 0.07 stations per km^2 in 2030 and 0.1 stations per km^2.

Note: [a, b, c] Chapter 6 provides sensitivity analyses with respect to these elements.

2.2. The reference policy scenario

The reference policy scenario is composed of the root assumptions detailed in the previous section and a set of currently- implemented land-use and transport policies, which are kept fixed throughout the study period 2018-2050. Hence, this reference scenario represents a "*business-as-usual*" (hereafter, BAU) path. The policy components of this scenario are presented in Table 2.4.

In transportation, a BAU path implies that the contribution of the Emission Trading Scheme (ETS) in the final price of gasoline remains fixed at the average value of 0.016 New Zealand dollars per litre of gasoline observed between the inauguration of the scheme in July 2010 and the base year of the study (2018). The same holds for all other tax components that make up the final price of gasoline such as the excise tax. Furthermore, a regional fuel tax, also a component of the final price of gasoline, is assumed to remain constant at NZD 0.115 per litre until 2050.

A BAU path also implies a fixed vehicle ownership tax that is not differentiated between conventional and electric vehicles. That tax is composed of three different charges: a registration fee (NZD 202.81 in 2018), a value-added tax paid on the purchase of a new vehicle (estimated at NZD 4 682 in 2018[7]) and an annual licensing fee. The first two components are converted to flat kilometre taxes, resulting in a rate of NZD 0.0244/km[8]. In contrast, the annual licensing fee is paid every year the car remains active in the fleet. It is therefore modelled as a fixed yearly cost.

Furthermore, under the BAU path, the current public transport fares in Auckland, as well as the road user fees that apply countrywide (NZD 0.06 per kilometre in 2018), remain constant. The density of electric vehicle recharging stations, estimated to be 0.0343 stations per km^2 of urban fabric in 2018, increases to 0.07 stations in 2030 and to 0.1 stations in 2050. Finally, the BAU path does not involve any ban of conventional vehicles.

In land use, a BAU path implies that all current urban development regulations remain fixed. The expansion of the current residential urban footprint, which is represented by the grey-coloured areas in Figure 2.6, takes place through the conversion of land that in year 2018 is labelled as "*future urban*". The latter is represented by the black-coloured areas in Figure 2.6 and is conceded for development in a pattern that mimics the existing one. This means that, in the BAU path, the proportion of land allocated to each development type (e.g. single-family detached, single-family attached and multifamily) in the newly developed areas is the average share of residential land occupied by each of these types in the existing residential footprint. Finally, in a BAU path all infrastructure, such as roads, schools and healthcare facilities, expands proportionately to existing infrastructure.

Figure 2.6. Current and future residential urban footprint of Auckland

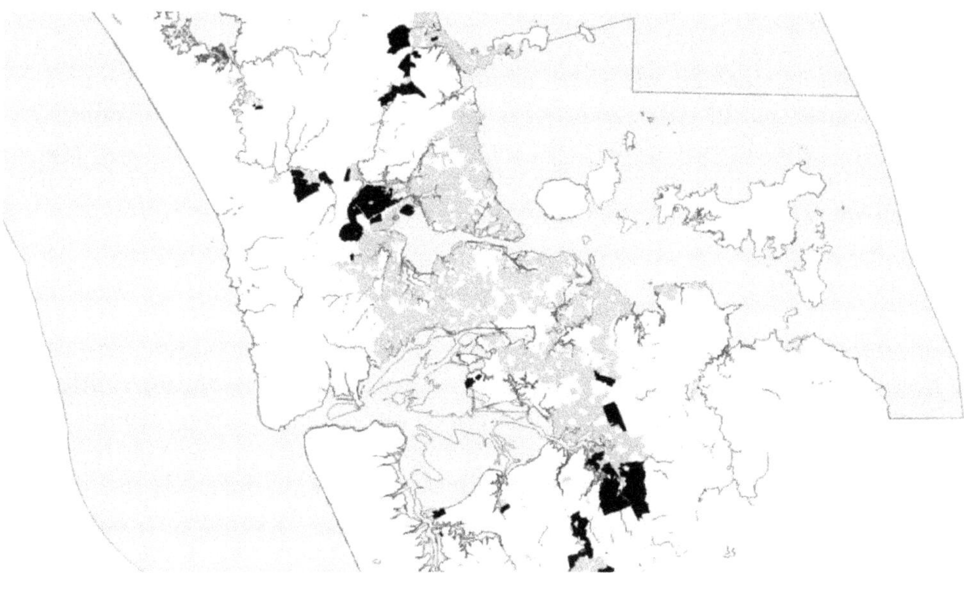

Note: Areas indicated by grey colour represent the current residential footprint; areas indicated by black represent land plots conceded for development between 2018 and 2050.
Source: Adapted by the authors from (Auckland Council, 2018[15]).

Table 2.4. The business-as-usual (BAU) policy package for the reference scenario.

Element	Assumptions
Standard tax components of electricity prices	VAT: remains fixed at 15% Excise tax: does not apply
Standard tax components of gasoline prices	VAT: remains fixed at 15% Excise tax: remains fixed at NZD 0.67/litre
Other tax components of gasoline prices	The ETS component of gasoline price remains fixed at its 2010-2018 average, i.e. NZD 0.016 per litre; A regional fuel tax of NZD 0.07 per litre is introduced and kept fixed throughout the study period.
Tax component of vehicle ownership	Annual licensing fee is kept constant at NZD 109.9 per year.
Vehicle depreciation per kilometre	Costs associated with purchasing a vehicle (including registration fee and VAT) are expressed in per kilometre terms. They remain fixed at NZD 0.186 per kilometre.
Road charges	Remain fixed at NZD 0.06 per kilometre in the entire study period.
Local road pricing	No measures are implemented.
Parking policies	On-street parking fees in Auckland CBD, expressed in real terms, are stable over time.
Public transport fares	Remain fixed in real terms.
Electric vehicle support measures	Electric vehicles are exempt from road charges up to 2030.
Residential footprint	All areas designated as *residential* in 2018 remain as such; Future urban areas are converted to residential at a steady rate; The development pattern in newly developed areas mimics that of existing residential areas; The development pattern in existing residential areas remains intact.

The reference scenario, which is comprised of the "root" assumptions and the BAU policy components, constitutes the benchmark against which *counterfactual* scenarios are evaluated. The components of this reference scenario are summarised in Table 2.4. All counterfactual scenarios include the same assumptions about population growth and technological progress in the EV industry as in the reference scenario (Table 2.2). However, in every counterfactual scenario the business-as-usual (BAU) policy scenario is replaced by an alternative policy scenario. The latter is a combination of *one or more* policy packages, which are presented in the following section.

2.3. Counterfactual policy packages

The selection of the counterfactual policy packages is motivated by the target of reducing emissions from urban transport. The selected policies lower emissions through different channels. Depending on the combination of the policy and the mechanism of emissions reductions, the shift towards low-carbon mobility may also generate various side benefits. For example, policies that reduce the number of private vehicles on the roads also reduce congestion, while policies that increase population density around employment zones can reduce travel distances (Ang and Marchal, 2013[16]).[9] Another criterion for the policies selected is also that they are compatible with the land-use and transport model, MOLES, used to run the policy simulations.

The first package entails policy components designed to **promote public transport over private vehicles** (hereafter referred to as the "***promote public transport***" policy package**)**. Policies in this package increase the fixed private costs of *both* ICE vehicles and EVs. This is done by increasing the annual circulation fees of these vehicles by NZD 2 000. The package also includes a substantial increase in the operational costs of private vehicles. Road charges are increased by NZD 0.5 per kilometre while a congestion charge scheme in the form of a double cordon toll surrounding the CBD and the isthmus area. The pricing

Figure 2.7. The areas densified under the four versions of the targeted densification package

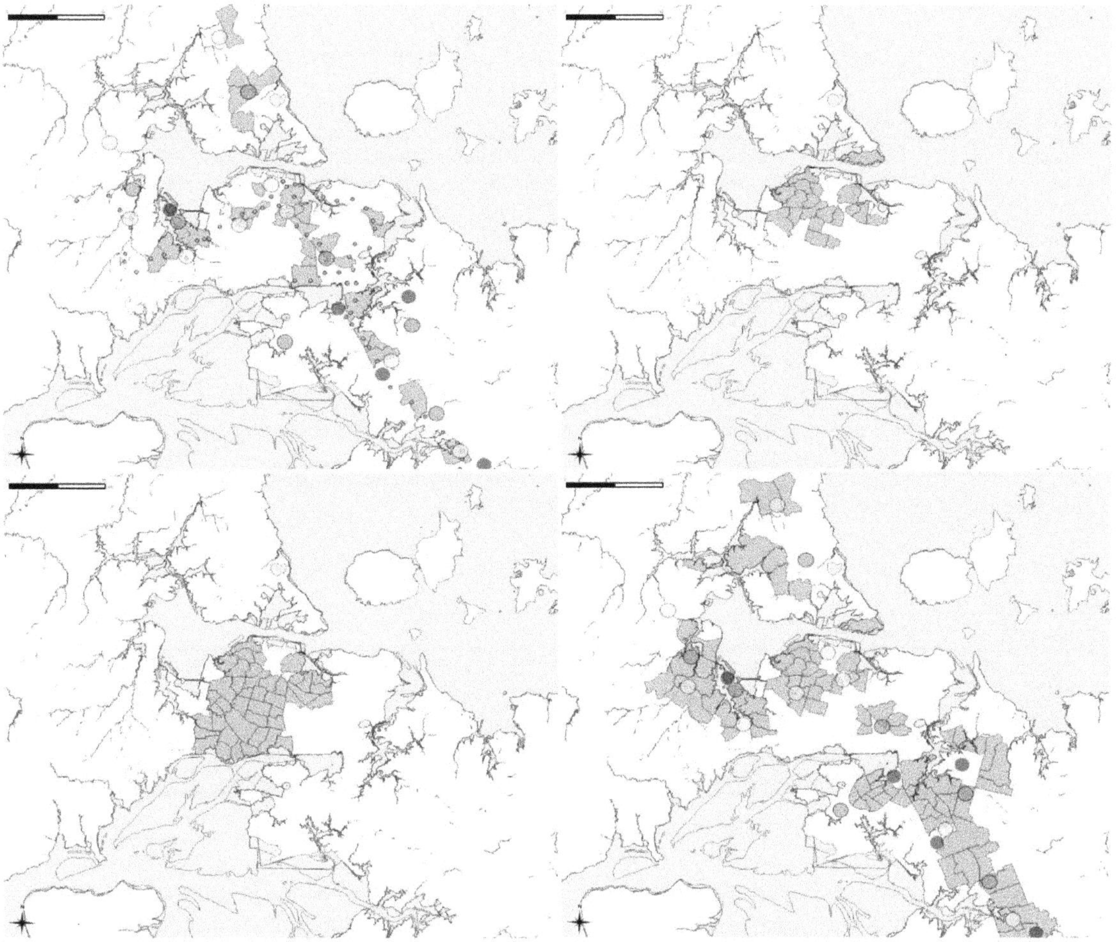

Note: Top left panel: transit-oriented densification; top right panel: densification around the Central Business District; bottom right panel: employment densification; bottom left panel: densification of the isthmus area. Orange dots represent major transport nodes (rail); Large grey and black dots represent hubs of all employment types; The zones where targeted densification takes place are designated with grey colour.
Source: Visualisation generated by the authors.

In order to examine the degree to which densification may help reduce emissions in urban areas, the study examines an alternative urban planning strategy, in which densification occurs exclusively in targeted areas. The study examines four **targeted densification** packages, each of them selecting the zones to be densified with a different criterion. The selected zones under each of these four packages are shown in Figure 2.7. The first targeted densification package, here referred to as "**transit-oriented densification**" and coded as TD1, selects areas of substantial density that lie close to large employment hubs and transit nodes. The second one, referred to as "**CBD-surrounding densification**" and coded as TD2, is a package that densifies low density areas surrounding the central business district. The third package, entitled "**densify isthmus**" and coded as TD3, selects all low-density areas in the entire inner core of Auckland as areas where densification may take place. Finally, the package entitled "**job-surrounding densification**" and coded as TD4, further densifies areas of already-considerable density surounding the largest employment hubs. Targeted densification packages intensify the growth of structural density, and therefore housing supply, in the selected zones. The associated building heights and coverage coefficients are provided in detail in Chapter 3.

Table 2.7. The "widespread densification" policy packages

Element	Assumptions
Existing residential footprint	Stays intact throughout the entire study horizon. Areas designated as "future urban" are conceded for residential development of relatively higher density; the development in *all* existing residential areas is densified by relaxing height restrictions and by reducing the minimum amount of backyard open space per m^2 of developed area (coverage coefficient).
New residential development	Future urban areas are conceded entirely for the development of multifamily housing.
Floor-to-area (FAR) ratio	Increases by 50% in all land plots reserved any type of residential development.
Coverage coefficient	Increases by 50% in all land plots reserved for any type of residential development.

Note: the rest of the 'root' assumptions remain as in Table 2.3.

Table 2.8. The "targeted densification" policy packages

Element	Assumptions
Floor-to-area (FAR) ratio	FAR ratio in the targeted area increases by 170% for residence types denoted as single-family housing in the benchmark, 290% for residence types denoted as mixed housing and 160% for residence types denoted as apartments.
Coverage coefficient	Coverage coefficient increases by 85% for residence types denoted as single-family and mixed housing in the benchmark, 50% for residence types denoted as apartments.

Note: the rest of the 'root' assumptions remain as in Table 2.3.

Interaction between different policies and policy types is an important feature of the study. Transport and land-use policies are not necessarily additive in their outcomes. Rather, they are subject to synergies and trade-offs. This necessitates an examination of different combinations of the policy packages presented in this chapter. That is provided in the results of the study, detailed in Chapter 5.

Notes

[1] Fixed *individual preference parameters* is a standard assumption in dynamic simulation or econometric models. It should be noted that the assumption of fixed preferences does not imply that any of the *individual choices* remains fixed over time. The latter evolve as economic constraints and incentives change over time. Stated differently, *preferences* refer to the technical parameters of the model that, along with other economic aspects (e.g. prices), affect the observable behaviour of individuals, i.e. the actual choices.

[2] Historically, technical progress in improving the fuel economy of ICE vehicles has been partly offset by preferences for larger and more powerful cars. Over the past thirty years, however, there has been a clear trend towards improving improved vehicle fuel economy. This has coincided with policy initiatives, which set technical and efficiency standards for new cars but vary at a national level. Since the New Zealand vehicle fleet is composed of imported cars, the majority of which are produced in Japan, changes to the fuel economy are affected by changes in the fuel economy of Japanese cars.

[3] The formula to calculate CO_2e emissions from electric buses is:

$$\frac{CO_2e}{km} = \frac{1}{R} \cdot \left(\frac{kWh}{km}\right) \cdot \left(\frac{CO_2e}{kWh}\right),$$

where R is the occupancy rate.

[4] This is calculated by dividing the total passenger kilometres driven by bus in 2018 with the estimated vehicle kilometres generated by buses. The latter is approximated by the ratio of the total litres of diesel consumed by buses in 2018 to the fuel economy of a representative bus.

[5] This is a limitation of the model, leading to an overestimation of emissions from public transport. That limitation should be considered in the evaluation of policies that increase public transport ridership in 2030 and 2050. However, the discrepancy is not sizeable, due to the assumption of public transport's gradual electrification.

[6] The benchmark year of the study is 2018. Where 2018 data is not available, data from the closest available year is used instead.

[7] The VAT paid on the purchase price of a new car (NZD 4 682) is calculated by multiplying the pre-tax price of an average new car in 2018, estimated at NZD 31 210, with the VAT of 15%.

[8] This is done by dividing the corresponding lump-sum fees by the assumed kilometric lifespan of a car (200 000 km).

[9] Chapter 3 provides a full discussion of the calculation of the welfare outcomes of each of these policy packages.

[10] For instance, the average annual wage in Sweden is approximately EUR 36 500, labour supply per worker is 1 609 hours per year, or approximately 201 days per year. That implies an average daily gross income of € 181.6. Assuming an average daily toll cost of EUR 2.9 (SEK 30) implies a daily cost of approximately 1.6% of gross income.

[11] The actual fares paid for a trip taken with public transport in Auckland depend on the number of zones the passenger traverses during the trip. That number correlates, but does not coincide, with trip distance. The subsidy reduces the per-zone price relative to the BAU by 80%. It should not be confused with a fixed subsidy per kilometre.

[12] For instance, densifying a 200 m^2 land plot, which is 50% covered by a five-storey building with the widespread densification program produces 625 m^2 of additional residential floor space. The corresponding increase for an identical land plot whose surface is covered by 30% by a two-storey building is 150 m^2.

References

Ang, G. and V. Marchal (2013), "Mobilising Private Investment in Sustainable Transport: The Case of Land-Based Passenger Transport Infrastructure", *OECD Environment Working Papers*, No. 56, OECD Publishing, Paris, https://dx.doi.org/10.1787/5k46hjm8jpmv-en. [16]

Auckland Council (2018), *Auckland Plan 2050*, http://www.aucklandplan.govt.nz. [15]

Auckland Council (2018), *Auckland Plan 2050 Evidence report: Demographic trends for Auckland: Data sources and findings*, Auckland Council, Auckland, https://www.aucklandcouncil.govt.nz/plans-projects-policies-reports-bylaws/our-plans-strategies/auckland-plan/about-the-auckland-plan/Evidence%20reports%20documents/evidence-report-demographics.pdf. [1]

Auckland Transport (2018), *Auckland's Low Emission Bus Roadmap.* [11]

Chediak, M. (2017), *The Latest Bull Case for Electric Cars: the Cheapest Batteries Ever*, Bloomberg, https://www.bloomberg.com/news/articles/2017-12-05/latest-bull-case-for-electric-cars-the-cheapest-batteries-ever. [3]

EPA (2018), *Fuel Economy Data*, https://www.fueleconomy.gov/feg/download.shtml. [5]

EVDB (2019), *Nissan Leaf price and specifications*, Electric Vehicle Database, https://ev-database.org/car/1106/Nissan-Leaf. [10]

IEA (2018), *Energy prices in national currency per unit.* [13]

IEA (2018), *Indices of energy prices by sector.* [14]

IEA (2017), *Energy Policies of IEA Countries - New Zealand*, International Energy Agency, http://www.iea.org/t&c/. [9]

Laffont, K. and E. Peirano (2013), *Annex to D3.1 - Technology Assessment Report: Demand-side Technologies: Electric Vehicles*, Technofi, http://www.e-highway2050.eu/fileadmin/documents/Results/D3/report_electric_vehicles.pdf. [2]

New Zealand Ministry of Transport (2017), *Transport Outlook: Future State.* [7]

New Zealand Transport Agency (2018), *New Zealand vehicle fleet open data sets*, https://www.nzta.govt.nz/resources/new-zealand-motor-vehicle-register-statistics/new-zealand-vehicle-fleet-open-data-sets/. [6]

Nykvist, B. and M. Nilsson (2015), "Rapidly falling costs of battery packs for electric vehicles", *Nature Climate Change*, http://dx.doi.org/10.1038/nclimate2564. [4]

Statistics New Zealand (2017), *Disposable income per person*, http://archive.stats.govt.nz/browse_for_stats/snapshots-of-nz/nz-social-indicators/Home/Standard%20of%20living/disp-income-pp.aspx. [12]

Transpower (2018), *Te Mauri Hiko - Energy Futures*, https://www.transpower.co.nz/sites/default/files/publications/resources/TP Energy Futures - Te Mauri Hiko 21 May%2718 - web.pdf. [8]

Annex 2.A. Note on different concepts of density

Two different concepts of density are used in this study: structural density and population density.

Structural density refers to the distribution of dwellings, building and residential floor space across the urban area. Two different measures of structural density are used: vertical density and horizontal density. Vertical density refers to building height and is measured through the floor-to-area ratio. The floor-to-area ratio is the relationship of the total amount of floor space to the parcel of land the building is located on. It is calculated as:

$$FAR = \frac{total\ floor\ area}{land\ area\ covered\ by\ buildings}$$

Horizontal density refers to the amount of backyard open space per m^2 of developed area. It is measured through the coverage coefficient, i.e. the share of a land plot's surface area occupied by the building footprint. It is calculated as:

$$Coverage\ coefficient = \frac{land\ area\ covered\ by\ buildings}{land\ area}$$

Population density refers to the distribution of population per unit of area. Three different measures of population are used: population density per square kilometre of land area; population density per square kilometre of built area and population density per square kilometre of floor space.

Chapter 3. Modelling transport and land use in Auckland

This chapter provides a non-technical description of the Multi-Objective Local Environmental Simulator (MOLES), i.e. the urban computable general equilibrium (CGE) model OECD has developed to evaluate the environmental and economic impact of land use and transport policies. The chapter focuses on the version of the model which has been tailored to Auckland. It details the behaviour of households and real-estate developers and elaborates on the way housing and land markets function in the model. It also describes the various outcomes of the modelling exercise, which include transport, emission, welfare, housing and fiscal indicators.

3.1. Overview of MOLES

The Multi-Objective Local Environmental Simulator (MOLES) is a multi-period urban Computable General Equilibrium (CGE) model developed by the OECD (Tikoudis and Oueslati, 2017[1]) to evaluate policy responses to scenarios in the spirit of those outlined in Chapter 2. It adopts features from traditional CGE models developed for national and international economies (*e.g.* clearing of multiple markets, atomistic behaviour of firms and households) and adjusts them to the scale of the urban economy, in which the markets for land, housing and transport play a key role. At the same time, MOLES imports a series of elements from microsimulation models in order to account for detailed behavioural mechanisms that cannot be represented in an aggregate model. In an urban environment, such mechanisms include, but are not limited to, the choice of the commuting route, the frequency of shopping and leisure trips and the decision to make a shopping detour during the course of a commuting trip.

Figure 3.1. The version of MOLES used in the current study

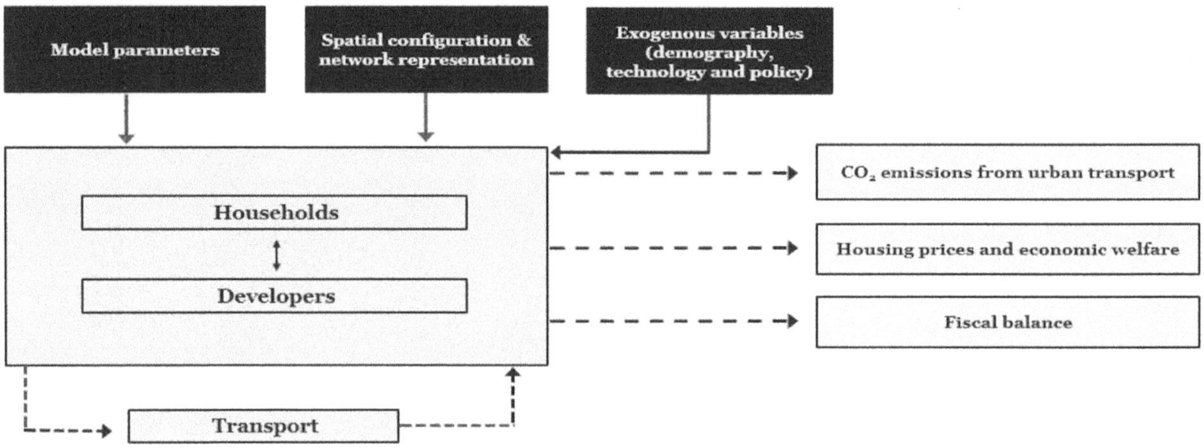

Note: Solid unidirectional arrows represent model inputs; bidirectional arrows represent model interactions; short-dashed arrows represent feedback effects; long-dashed arrows represent model outputs.
Source: Visualisation generated by the authors; for full model documentation please see Tikoudis and Oueslati (2017[2]).

The general structure of the model is presented in Figure 3.1. The core of MOLES contains a series of behavioural equations that determine the aggregate housing supply and demand for each residential type available in each zone considered in the model. In turn, these aggregate variables are computed using an iterative technique. That is, MOLES considers every feasible combination of a residential location, a job location, a vehicle type and a commuting mode (hereafter, alternative). For each such combination, it computes how individuals that commit to that choice split their expenditure between housing and other types of consumption and how they allocate their time. The associated calculations respect budget and time constraints that are formed using expected travel times and costs. The supply side of housing is driven by a profit-maximising construction sector which, in the context of the present study, is heavily regulated. That is, aggregate housing supply is determined completely by the background regulatory mechanisms that dictate building height and the percentage of the developable land that can be occupied by residential constructs. The core model equilibrates the housing markets by calculating the housing price that would eliminate excess demand or supply for any housing type in any model zone.

The *transport module* uses the resulting distribution of the population across residential zones and job hubs to predict its mobility pattern. The module uses statistical techniques designed to generate trips during the on-peak and off-peak period of weekdays, as well as during weekends. It then uses these techniques to compute the resulting traffic from those commuting, shopping and leisure trips. Subsequently, the module assigns the resulting traffic volumes in the various parts of the transport networks and updates the travel speeds in them. Finally, the updated speeds are used to provide new estimates for the annual expected travel time and cost associated with any joint choice of residential location, job location and vehicle type. These updates are then passed as feedback from the transport module to the model's core. That is solved again in order to provide a new distribution of the population across residential zones and employment hubs and to update the prices that clear all housing markets. MOLES keeps on iterating between its core and its transport module until the feedback from the latter induces only negligible changes in the output of the former. When this occurs, MOLES has converged.

Figure 3.1 suggests, the outcome of the simulation exercise depends partly on the exogenous model inputs. These include the values of model parameters that remain fixed throughout all time periods; the values of exogenous and policy variables, which may change across time periods but remain fixed within a given period; and the spatial configuration, which is retrieved from GIS data.

3.2. Model inputs

In order for MOLES to be initialised, the exogenous variables and the policy parameters have to be inserted in the model. As explained in Chapter 2, these inputs constitute a scenario, which can be in the form of a reference scenario or a counterfactual scenario. Furthermore, MOLES requires sufficient information about the spatial configuration of the examined urban area and its transport networks. These inputs, which are described in detail in Chapter 4, include: a representation of the highway, urban road and public transport networks; a partition of the urban area in zones; and a representation of the key loci of economic activity, such as employment areas, major shopping hubs and leisure locations. Finally, the model parameters need to be given numerical values. These parameters govern households' responses to changes in prices and the non-pecuniary elements that affect their budget and time constraints, choices and, ultimately, their well-being. That is, the model parameters determine how households adjust: their overall consumption; the size, type and location of their residence, therefore their housing expenditure; the choice of owning a private vehicle or not; and their mobility patterns. The *mobility patterns* encompass the mode and route households choose for their commuting, leisure and shopping trips, as well as the chosen frequency of all non-commuting trips. Due to the important role parametric specification plays in determining these values, the calibration of the model (*i.e.* the selection of model parameters so that the model predictions fit the data) is discussed separately in Chapter 4.

Figure 3.2. Residential zones and employment hubs in the study

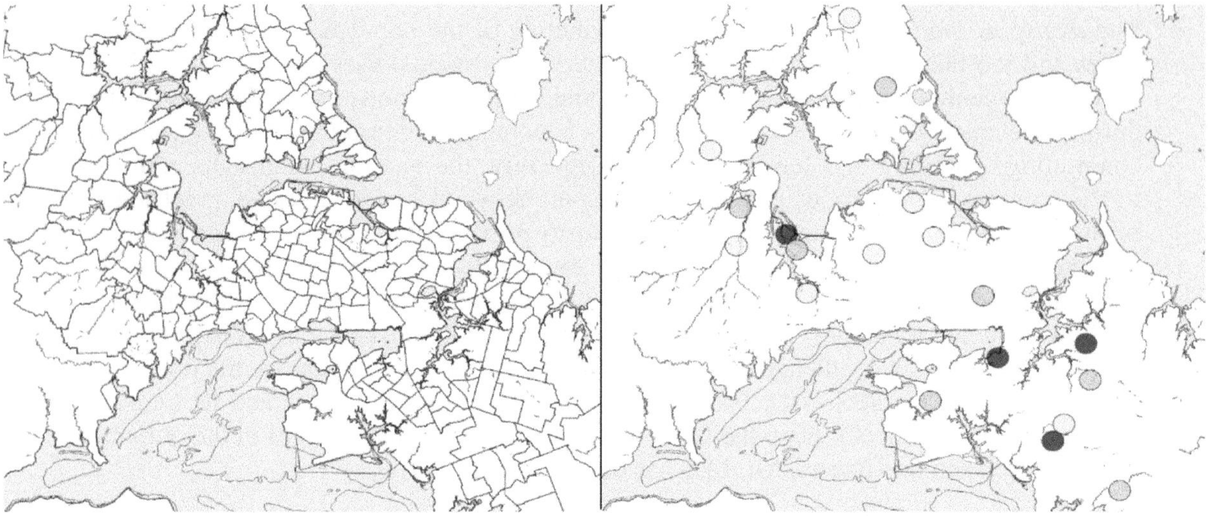

Note: Left panel: residential zones; right panel: employment hubs. For more information about the construction of model residential zones and employment hubs the reader is referred to Chapter 4 of this study.
Source: Visualisation generated by the authors.

3.3. Core model: individual behaviour

The core module of MOLES is a mathematical representation of the market interactions taking place between households and real-estate developers. These interactions determine housing and land prices, as well as the allocation of population across the different zones of the city.

Individuals have some *initial expectations* regarding their annual transport expenditure, as well as the time they will have to spend on the road for any locational choice they make. Based on these expectations, households decide in which zone they are going to reside and to which employment hub they are going to supply labour. This choice is displayed in Figure 3.2, which shows the candidate residential zones (left panel) and employment locations (right panel) in the case study presented in this report. Simultaneously, households choose the type and size of their residence, as well as their consumption expenditure. They also decide whether they are going to own a private vehicle and, if yes, whether that vehicle is going to be a conventional ICE vehicle or an EV.

These *primary choices*, which are summarised in Table 3.1, have to be consistent with the households' budget and time constraint. Accounting for a valid budget constraint means that MOLES considers only options (alternatives) guaranteeing that a household's annual spending in consumption, housing and transport equals its annual income. The model allows all realistic substitution patterns to emerge during that choice. This means that households can control their housing expenditure by choosing to live in a less accessible area, in which land prices are typically lower. Alternatively, they may respond to house price raises by adjusting the size of their residence or by lowering their consumption.

Table 3.1. Primary choices made by households in MOLES

Variable	Description and options
Residential location	In which residential zone to reside (195 zones)
Residential type [a]	In which housing type to live (single family detached, single family attached, multifamily apartment building)
Employment location	In which employment hub to work (22 hubs)
Vehicle ownership	Whether to own a vehicle or not
Vehicle type [b]	Internal combustion engine (ICE) or electric vehicle (EV)
Residential size	Residential floor space (m^2)
Consumption	Annual spending excluding housing goods and transport

Note: [a] Further detail follows; [b] applicable only if the vehicle ownership decision is positive.

Furthermore, MOLES explicitly models the time constraint, in the sense that the sum of the working day duration, daily leisure and the average time spent on the various types of trips per day cannot exceed the 24-hour daily time endowment. As it is the case with the budget constraint, MOLES allows substitution patterns to emerge also through the time constraint. This means that households can choose to live at relatively more accessible locations if their valuation of leisure time is high, thereby substituting monetary resources for leisure time. If the valuation of leisure time is low, the reverse could happen. However, every such trade-off can only take place if it obeys the *budgetary* and *time constraints* of households.

The primary choices of Table 3.1 contain the car ownership and vehicle type decisions. These decisions, together with the level of vehicle utilisation, bear a significant environmental importance: they determine whether the annual number of kilometres is going to be traversed with a relatively clean or polluting mode of transport.

By choosing residential size, type and location, households form the aggregate housing demand across urban space. That demand is the total number of m^2 of floor space from each residential type demanded in each zone of the model. The next section discusses the supply side of the housing market.

3.4. Core model: real estate developers

The *supply side* of housing is represented by the housing development sector, which operates under the constraints set out by land-use regulations. This sector can re-develop existing land and convert land to the various housing types the model considers. These housing types differ with respect to: (i) their *structural density*, which is the average number of m^2 of residential space the housing type yields for every m^2 of its building footprint; (ii) the *coverage coefficient*, which is the average percentage of the land plot occupied by the footprint of the building; (iii) whether they are attached or detached. The left panel of Figure 3.3 shows the residential development pattern in Auckland, which comprises five predominant residential types. The right panel of the same figure displays how these types are represented in the model by three aggregate residential types: attached single-family housing, detached single-family housing and multi-family appartment buildings.

Figure 3.3. Residential types and their representation in MOLES

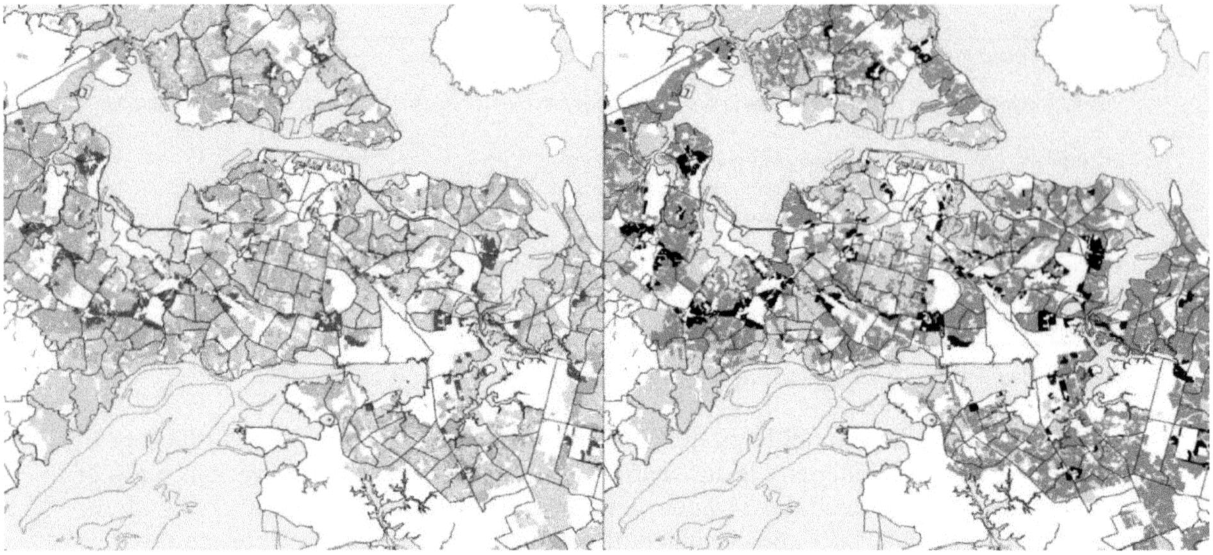

Note: Left panel: the footprint of the five predominant residential housing types in Auckland; right panel: model representation of the residential development pattern. Light grey: detached single family housing; dark grey: attached single family housing; black: multi-family apartment buildings.
Source: Visualisation generated by the authors.

That conversion takes place according to a profit maximization plan and complies with the regulatory framework that applies in every residential zone. The former postulate implies that, in any given land plot, developers erect the housing type that provides the maximum profit. The latter postulate implies that, if land-use and housing development regulations are strict, the overall development pattern in a city is predetermined (at least to a large extent) by that regulatory framework. The latter is embodied in the scenario the model is provided with.

Table 3.2. Housing types in the reference and widespread densification policy packages.

	Reference		Widespread densification policy package	
Residential type	**Average FAR [a] ratio**	**Coverage [b] coefficient**	**Average FAR [a] ratio**	**Coverage [b] coefficient**
Detached single family	1.50	0.30	2.25	0.450
Attached single family	2.25	0.35	3.38	0.525
Apartment	5.00	0.50	7.5	0.750

Note: [a] Shorthand notation for floor-to-area ratio, i.e. the number of m^2 of residential floor space corresponding to one m^2 of built footprint; [b] the share of land plot's surface occupied by the building footprint.

Table 3.3. Housing types in the targeted densification policy packages.

Residential type	Average FAR [a] ratio	Coverage [b] coefficient
Dense type 1	4.00	0.55
Dense type 2	6.50	0.65
Dense type 3	8.00	0.75

Note: [a] Shorthand notation for floor-to-area ratio, i.e. the number of m^2 of residential floor space corresponding to one m^2 of built footprint; [b] the share of land plot's surface occupied by the building footprint.

3.5. Core model: market clearing in land and housing markets

MOLES solves for the housing prices that equalize the aggregate housing demand, i.e. the sum of demand for residential floor space, with the aggregate housing supply, i.e. the supply of residential floor space by real estate developers.[1] At the same time, MOLES solves for the land prices that equalize aggregate land demand with aggregate land supply.

The housing and land market clearing imply that every locational advantage a zone possesses will result in higher housing and land prices. Thus, housing in urban zones characterised by higher accessibility, lower levels of air pollution and noise, as well as proximity to environmental amenities (e.g. sea view, short distance from recreational areas) will be relatively more expensive and *vice versa*. For more information regarding the fit of relative housing prices predicted by MOLES to the actual relative prices of housing in Auckland, the reader is referred to the calibration of the model in Chapter 4. Taking consideration of the land market clearing implies that the flow of land value that remains within the local economy, i.e. the land revenue that returns to local property owners, fits the corresponding number observed in data.

The core part of MOLES depicted in Figure 3.1 is solved for assumed travel times and costs that deviate from the resulting ones. If the anticipated times and costs are too low, they will generate more travel demand than initially expected. Thus, the resulting traffic volumes will be larger, implying that the resulting travel times and costs will be larger than the anticipated ones. A similar logic holds *vice versa*. The peripheral *transport* module, which is connected with dashed arrows with the core of the model in Figure 3.1, corrects these expectations. The next section provides a non-technical summary of its function.

3.6. Transport module: route choice, traffic assignment and update of travel times and costs

The core solution of MOLES determines the population density in each urban zone and the employment level in each employment hub, but does not model explicitly the mobility pattern of households in the examined urban area. Stated differently, it determines the long-run location decisions of households (e.g. where to live, where to work) for any beliefs they may have regarding the travel times and transport costs associated with any such decision. These beliefs may be incorrect in the short run (e.g. due to imperfect information, change of habits). However, MOLES assumes that in the long-run households are able to make informed decisions based on the actual average travel time and cost they will face for every long-run decision they make.

The centroids of residential model zones, displayed in the upper left panel of Figure 3.4, are used as starting points to simulate commuting trips, home-based shopping trips and leisure trips. Similarly, the employment and leisure hubs, represented by the dots in the upper and lower right panels of Figure 3.4, are used as destination points in commuting and leisure trips, respectively. Finally, the shopping hubs, shown in the lower left panel of Figure 3.4 serve as destinations of home-based shopping trips or as interim stops in shopping detours embodied in commuting trips. Table 3.4 summarizes the four types of trips the model considers. Summary statistics and further detail on the various data sources used in the study are presented in Chapter 4.

Schooling trips were omitted due to computation constraints and as they contribute much less to carbon emissions than commuting, shopping and leisure trips. This is expanded on in Chapter 4.

Figure 3.4. Origins and destinations of commuting, shopping and leisure trips in MOLES

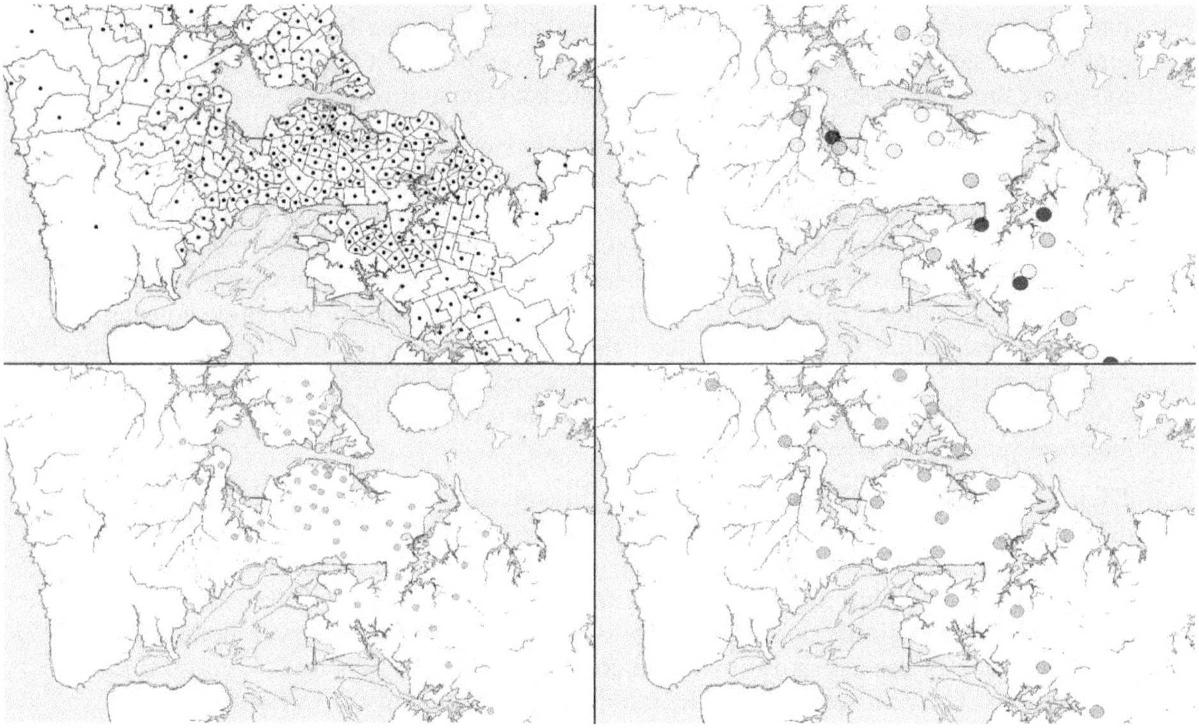

Note: Upper left panel: residential zone centroids functioning as origins of commuting trips (equivalently, destinations of home returning trips); Upper right panel: employment hubs, functioning as destinations of commuting trips (origins of home returning trips); Lower left panel: shopping hubs, functioning as destinations of shopping trips or detour stops during commuting trips; Lower right panel: representation of leisure locations, functioning as destinations of leisure trips.
Source: Visualisation generated by the authors.

Table 3.4. Types of trips in the MOLES application for Auckland

Commuting trip	A trip starting from the centroid of a residential location, ending in one of the employment nodes, and *vice versa*, without an interim stop.
Commuting trip with a shopping detour	A trip starting from the centroid of a residential location and stopping to an interim shopping location before reaching an employment node (and *vice versa*).
Home-based shopping trip	A trip starting from the centroid of a residential location, ending in one of the shopping locations, and *vice versa*.
Leisure-trip	A trip starting from the centroid of a residential location, ending in one of the leisure locations, and *vice versa*.

Figure 3.5. Transport network representation in MOLES

Note: Upper left panel: urban road network; Upper right panel: urban road network with a grid; Lower left panel: highway network; Lower right panel: public transport network.
Source: Visualisation generated by the authors.

In order to simulate any of the trips displayed in Table 3.4, MOLES uses three types of network representations: (i) a simplified version of the actual network of urban roads of low or medium capacity, consisting of 266 artificial nodes and 402 artificial links; (ii) a simplified version of the actual highway network (117 nodes, 127 links); and (iii) a representation of the public transport system (445 nodes, 685 links). These representations are shown in Figure 3.5. Then, MOLES simulates routes using the urban and the highway network, i.e. it generates routes for urban driving, highway driving, as well as hybrid routes in which the two types of driving are combined. All urban, highway and hybrid routes are available to those that own a private vehicle. Furthermore, MOLES uses the representation of the public transport system to simulate routes making use of public transport modes.

Subsequently, MOLES considers three separate statistical models for the choice of routes in daily trips. The first one, represented by Figure 3.6, regards the choice of a commuting route (urban, highway, hybrid or public transport) from a set of candidates. Some of these candidate routes are not compatible with a shopping detour. In that case, none of the shopping hubs shown in lower left panel of Figure 3.4 can be reached without a major deviation from the commuting route. An example is the candidate route R_2 in Figure 3.6, which serves as a pure commuting route. The rest of candidate commuting routes are compatible with shopping detours, i.e. one or more shopping locations lies at striking distance from some point within them. If the commuter decides to combine the candidate route with a shopping detour to a compatible shopping hub, the generalised cost of the trip increases accordingly. That accounts for the additional pecuniary and time costs the detour implies. However, the econometric model for the choice of commuting route accounts also for the additional utility derived from shopping detours. That additional utility correlates with the relative attractiveness of each shopping hub. The model yields choice probabilities for the most attractive routes that lead from any residential location (origin) to any employment location (destination).

Figure 3.6. Commuting route choice in MOLES

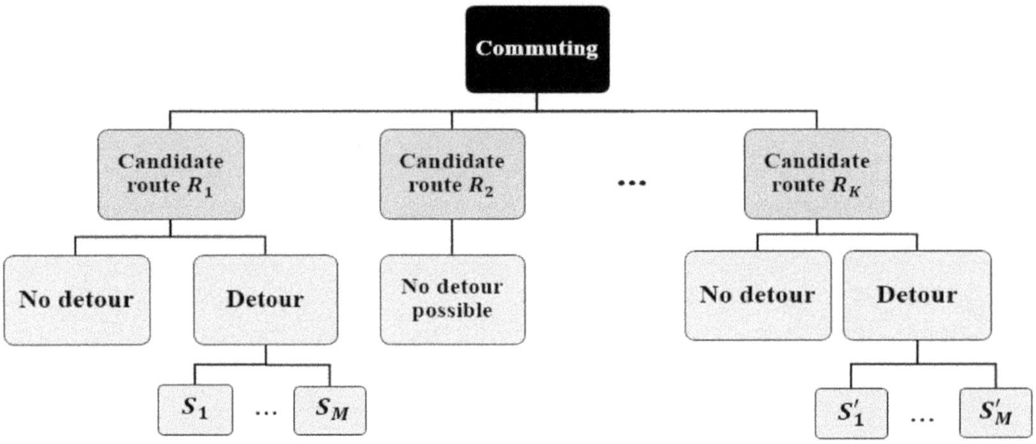

Note: Candidate route R_2 is not compatible with a commuting detour, as no shopping hub can be accessed without a major deviation from it.
Source: Visualisation generated by the authors.

The two econometric models that are used to simulate, respectively, the households' behaviour in home-based shopping and leisure trips are similar and therefore represented schematically with a single graph in Figure 3.7. At any period considered in the analysis (see below), an individual makes a choice between staying at home and engaging in a shopping (respectively, leisure) trip. If the choice is the latter one, the individual chooses one of the shopping (leisure) hubs shown in the lower left (lower right) panel of Figure 3.4. Different hubs yield different levels of utility. That allows the statistical model to approximate the relative attractiveness of each shopping or leisure hub, which is empirically observed.

The last step in the choice process involves the selection of route from home to the location of the shopping (leisure) hub selected in the previous stage. In most of the cases, the available routes, displayed at the bottom level of Figure 3.7, are served by public transport or have to be traversed with a private vehicle. However, in some cases the trip's destination, i.e. the shopping (leisure) hub, lies at the vicinity of household's location. In these cases, soft-mobility options are added to the choice set associated to that origin-destination pair.

An example of such a soft-mobility option is the alternative coded as R^*_{22}, whose presence in Figure 3.7 reflects the proximity of location L_2 to the home location of the individual taking the trip. Once a route is chosen, utility adjusts to account for its pecuniary cost and time. The choice of route implies the choice of the underlying transport mode, thus utility adjusts also to account for mode characteristics. A final look to Figure 3.7 shows that the underlying statistical model explains, jointly, the trip frequency, the choice of destination and the route used to access that destination. In that sense, individuals are more likely to engage in a shopping (leisure) trip the larger the accessibility, i.e. the smaller the generalised costs of accessing the most desirable locations from their home's location.

Figure 3.7. Home-based shopping and leisure trips in MOLES

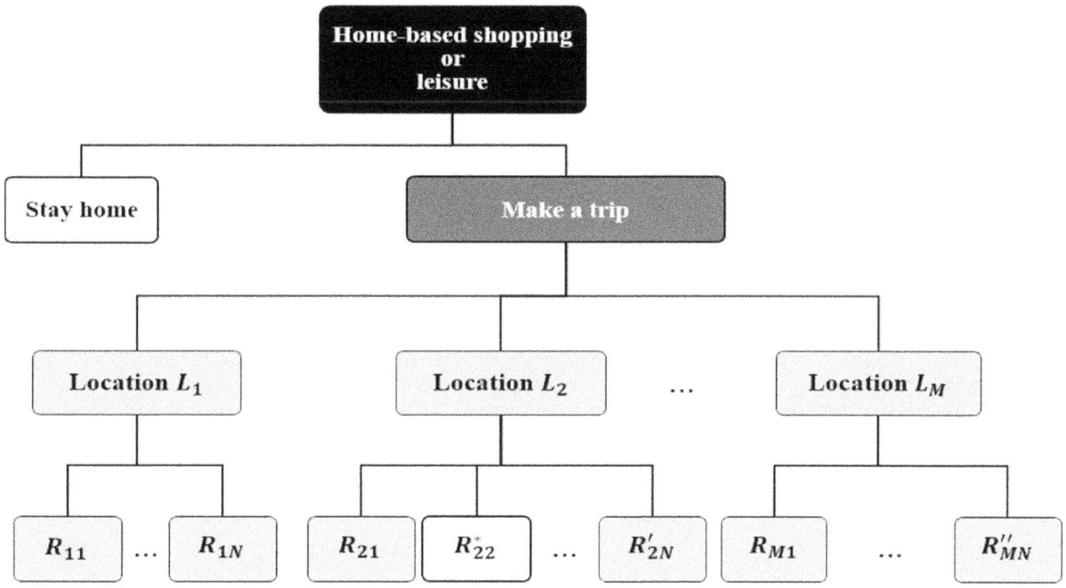

Source: Visualisation generated by the authors.

The total number of road users for each such origin-destination pair is known, i.e. it is the output of the MOLES core module. Thus, the average level of commuting traffic in each urban, highway and public transport route of Figure 3.5 can be computed by knowing the associated trip and route choice probabilities. MOLES generates a temporal variation in traffic by decomposing a period of one week into a two-day interval (weekend) and a sequence of on-peak and off-peak intervals, which succeed each other during the days between Monday and Friday. In that sense, route choice probabilities vary across the three representative periods composing a week, as shown in Table 3.5.

Table 3.5. Time periods in MOLES application for Auckland

On-peak period	All weekdays from 07:00 to 10:00 and from 16:30 to 20:00.
Off-peak period	All weekdays from 20:00 to 07:00 and from 10:00 to 16:30.
Weekends	Any time of the day during weekends.

Using these probabilities, highway traffic is allocated across the highway links shown in the lower left panel of Figure 3.5. Similarly, the traffic generated in urban and public transport routes is allocated across the rectangular cells (1.8 km × 1.8km) of the grid displayed in the upper right panel of Figure 3.5. Each of those cells can be viewed as a homogeneous area, in which the total traffic volume is the total number of passenger kilometres generated by public transport and privately owned vehicles. The total road capacity in the area is approximated by the percentage of land surface allocated to road infrastructure. The technical details of computing the level of traffic in links and grid cells from the traffic levels in routes are presented in Tikoudis and Oueslati (2017[1]).

3.7. Model outputs

Upon convergence of the core model and the transport module, the total fuel and electricity consumption and the fiscal and welfare implications of each of the scenarios are computed.

3.7.1. Transport sector outcomes and emissions

The *total fuel consumption* of ICE vehicles is computed using the number of kilometres they travel, on the highways and within the urban network. These kilometres are multiplied by the fuel consumption per kilometre. Equivalently, they are divided by the fuel economy, which is the inverse of fuel consumption. That is:

$$\text{Fuel Consumption (ICE)} = \frac{\text{ICE vehicle km urban}}{\text{Fuel Economy Urban (ICE)}} + \frac{\text{ICE vehicle km highway}}{\text{Fuel Economy Highway (ICE)}}$$

The *total CO_2e emissions* from ICE vehicle use is the product of total litres of fuel consumption and the carbon content per litre of fuel[2]:

$$\text{CO}_2\text{e (ICE)} = \text{Fuel Consumption (ICE)} \times \frac{\text{kg CO}_2\text{e}}{\text{lt}}$$

The *total electricity consumption of EVs* is computed using the number of kilometres they travel in the two networks (highways, urban roads). These kilometres are multiplied by the EV electricity consumption per km (kWh/km) in the two types of driving (highway, urban). That is:

$$\text{Electricity Consumption (EV)} = \text{EV km Urban} \times \left(\frac{\text{kWh}}{\text{km}}\right)_\text{U} + \text{EV km Highway} \times \left(\frac{\text{kWh}}{\text{km}}\right)_\text{H}$$

where the subscripts U, H stand for urban and highway, respectively.

The *total CO_2e emissions of EV use* is the product of electricity consumption and the carbon content embodied in each unit of energy, i.e. the *carbon intensity of the electricity generation sector*. That is:

$$CO_2e(EV) = \text{Electricity Consumption (EV)} \times \frac{\text{kg } CO_2e}{\text{kWh}}$$

The total *CO_2e emissions from the use of public transport modes* is calculated directly from the number of passenger kilometres (pkm) using rail and bus. These are multiplied by the carbon content of a passenger kilometre in rail and bus, respectively. That is:

$$CO_2e(PT) = \text{Bus pkm} \times \left(\frac{\text{kg } CO_2e}{\text{pkm}}\right)_B + \text{Rail pkm} \times \left(\frac{\text{kg } CO_2e}{\text{pkm}}\right)_R$$

where PT stands for public transport, pkm stands for passenger kilometres and the subscripts B and R stand for bus and rail, respectively.

The emissions from ICE vehicles, EVs and public transport modes change across different periods of the study. In the context of this study, this means that the above outcomes differ between 2018, 2030 and 2050. This happens because of three reasons. First, total transport activity changes across these time points, as population increases and individuals may make different transport-related choices. That affects the total kilometres travelled by ICE vehicles, EVs, as well as the passenger kilometres travelled using bus and rail. The second reason is that the energy efficiency of private vehicles and the carbon intensity of public transport change over time. ICE vehicles become more fuel efficient, i.e. they require less fuel and thus emit less carbon per kilometre. EVs become also more energy efficient, i.e. consume less electricity and thus have a smaller carbon footprint per kilometre. Public transport is gradually electrified over the course of the study period (2018-2050). Furthermore, the electricity use of an electric bus per kilometre falls as buses become more energy efficient. Finally, the CO_2e emissions from transport-related electricity consumption depend on the carbon intensity of the electricity-generation sector. The emissions per kilometre of ICE vehicles and EVs are presented in Chapter 2.

An important transport-related outcome is travel time. If a policy reduces congestion, travel times decrease, leaving households with more leisure time. This increases their well-being insofar they value leisure time. In reality, but also in the modelling exercise, individuals value leisure time higher on working days than on days off. This is because spare time is, in general, scarcer during weekdays. Therefore, reduced commuting times can significantly increase welfare.

3.7.2. Social value of carbon reduction

The primary motivation of the policies this report explores is the reduction of greenhouse gas emissions. Therefore, the social benefit of carbon reduction is taken into explicit account. This is calculated as the product of the total emission reductions a policy yields (relative to emissions in the reference scenario) and the estimated marginal damage of carbon dioxide emissions, i.e. the social cost of carbon (SCC). The associated welfare change from the reduction of carbon emissions, induced by a policy, is:

$$\Delta W_{CO2} = \Delta E_{CO2} \times SCC$$

The social cost of carbon evolves over time. This study assumes a SCC that is a weighted average of two values proposed by the US EPA (2017[3]): a value produced with a 2.5% annual discount rate (US$ 73 per ton in 2030, US$ 95 per ton in 2050) and a value produced with 3% discount rate, but under the assumption that extreme events have a high impact (US$ 152 per ton in 2030, US$ 212 per ton in 2050). Weighting the two proposals equally yields a SCC of US$ 112.5 per ton in 2030 and US$ 153.5 in 2050.

3.7.3. Impacts through housing prices

The land-use and transport policies examined in the report cause changes in the urban form, alter the distribution of population across space and affect housing prices. Also, the densification policies analysed in the study affect the proportion at which residential floor space and backyard open space will be consumed in each type of residential development.

Direct welfare impact of a policy

The direct welfare change of a policy is the difference in well-being (utility) expressed in monetary terms. It can be (roughly) expressed as:

$$\Delta W_{Direct} = \frac{W(P_H^1, TT^1, TC^1, RB^1) - W(P_H^0, TT^0, TC^0, RB^0)}{MUI}$$

where W is the level of well-being captured by the model. That depends on housing prices (P_H), travel times and costs (TT, TC) and the proportion at which residential and backyard spaces can be consumed. Since policies may change any, or all, of the above, they directly affect well-being. Well-being (utility) is expressed in non-monetary terms (utils), thus the direct welfare change is not monetized. It is converted to monetary units by dividing the change in utility (numerator) by the marginal utility of money (utils/NZD).[3]

3.7.4. Implicit fiscal effects

The fiscal policy instruments examined in the study, such as the fuel taxes, have tax bases that are directly affected by changes in the values of these instruments. For instance, two of the policy packages examined in the study (see "Promote public transport" and "Promote EVs") largely affect the tax base of the fuel tax.

In reality, the policy instruments included in the study affect also a series of tax bases that are not modelled explicitly. For example, the labour income tax base may be negatively affected by the increase of the kilometre tax, the fuel tax or from the adjustment of any instrument that increases the cost of a commuting trip. The distortionary impact of any such change on economic efficiency has been examined in relevant literature (Parry and Bento, 2001[4]; Parry and Bento, 2002[5]; Tikoudis, Verhoef and van Ommeren, 2015[6]; Tikoudis, 2019[7]). Other tax bases that may be affected form the adjustment of transport-related taxes, include the property tax base, although the negative impact is expected to be much smaller (Tikoudis, Verhoef and van Ommeren, 2018[8]).

The distortionary impact of negative tax interactions is not modelled explicitly. Instead, this is accounted for through an explicit weighting of the tax revenue using the *marginal cost of public funds* (MCF). The value of MCF used in the study is 1.10. This imposes an additional cost of 10% beyond the simple transfer of funds, when raising revenue from households to government. The study weights any change in the total tax revenue with the reciprocal of MCF in order to account for the negative tax interactions. The monetized welfare impact from the fiscal adjustments is:

$$\Delta W_{Fiscal} = \frac{(\Delta R_{tax} + \Delta R_{fares})}{MCF}$$

where ΔR_{tax} is the change in total tax revenue and ΔR_{fares} the change in total revenue from public transport fares.

3.7.5. Total welfare impact

The total welfare impact of a policy is composed of its direct welfare impact, its implicit fiscal effect and its social value of carbon reduction. The numbers reported in the study follow the convention:

$$\Delta W_{Total} = \Delta W_{Direct} + \Delta W_{Fiscal} + \Delta W_{CO2}$$

3.7.6. Non-modelled wider benefits

There are also other, broader benefits of the low-carbon transition which are not explicitly considered in the analysis. For example, a shift towards low-carbon transport improves air quality and reduces noise which has implications for welfare. These benefits are not included in the welfare calculations. Additionally, the health benefits of a shift towards active modes of travel such as biking or walking are not considered.

Notes

[1] Like every Computable General Equilibrium (CGE) model, MOLES assumes an instant adjustment of markets to exogenous shocks that affect the demand or the supply side. In that sense, housing markets clear instantly when regulations that affect housing supply change. This could be considered as a somewhat unrealistic assumption. Usually, property takes time to develop, e.g. 3 to 5 years to complete a development, and to sell. However, the multi-period version of MOLES used in this report assumes two large adjustment periods (see Chapter 5): the mid-term (2018-2030) and the long-run (2030-2050). These periods are long enough for all the relevant price adjustment mechanisms to be manifested.

[2] As explained in Chapter 2 data on diesel cars were not of sufficient quality to be included in the econometric analysis. Instead, the evolution of the fuel economy of diesel cars is assumed to follow the trajectory as gasoline and hybrid cars do.

[3] For the full technical documentation, see Tikoudis and Oueslati (2017[1]).

References

Parry, I. and A. Bento (2002), “Estimating the Welfare Effect of Congestion Taxes: The Critical Importance of Other Distortions within the Transport System”, *Journal of Urban Economics*, Vol. 51, pp. 339-365, http://dx.doi.org/10.1006rjuec.2001.2248. [5]

Parry, I. and A. Bento (2001), “Revenue Recycling and the Welfare Effects of Road Pricing”, *Scandinavian Journal of Economics*, Vol. 103/4, pp. 645-671. [4]

Tikoudis, I. (2019), “Second-Best Road Taxes in Polycentric Networks with Distorted Labor Markets”, *Scandinavian Journal of Economics*, http://dx.doi.org/10.1111/sjoe.12322. [7]

Tikoudis, I. and W. Oueslati (2017), “Multi-objective local environmental simulator (MOLES 1.0): Model specification, algorithm design and policy applications”, *OECD Environment Working Papers*, No. 122, OECD Publishing, Paris, http://dx.doi.org/10.1787/151cf08a-en. [1]

Tikoudis, I. and W. Oueslati (2017), “Multi-objective local environmental simulator (MOLES 1.0): Model specification, algorithm design and policy applications”, *OECD Environment Working Papers*, No. 122, OECD Publishing, Paris, https://dx.doi.org/10.1787/151cf08a-en. [2]

Tikoudis, I., E. Verhoef and J. van Ommeren (2018), “Second-best urban tolls in a monocentric city with housing market regulations”, *Transportation Research Part B: Methodological*, Vol. 117, http://dx.doi.org/10.1016/j.trb.2018.08.014. [8]

Tikoudis, I., E. Verhoef and J. van Ommeren (2015), “On revenue recycling and the welfare effects of second-best congestion pricing in a monocentric city”, *Journal of Urban Economics*, Vol. 89, http://dx.doi.org/10.1016/j.jue.2015.06.004. [6]

US EPA (2017), *The Social Cost of Carbon: Estimating the Benefits of Reducing Greenhouse Gas Emissions*, US Environmental Protection Agency, https://19january2017snapshot.epa.gov/climatechange/social-cost-carbon_.html. [3]

Chapter 4. Data and model calibration in the Auckland case study

This chapter provides a navigation of the various data sources and presents the model calibration. The first section describes the data sources, which include a travel survey conducted in New Zealand, geo-spatial data, New Zealand fleet registration data and Google API data on travel times. The chapter describes and visualises how land use and travel survey data are combined to create a stylised representation of residential and employment locations in Auckland. The second section, provides detail on the calibration of the model including the way households spend their income and allocate their time, as well as their travel behaviour and its elasticity to price and income changes. These values are important as they provide evidence of the adaptation of MOLES to Auckland and a link to the general empirical regularities reported in the literature.

4.1. Data sources and processing

4.1.1. GIS data

The study makes extensive use of Geographic Information System (GIS) data. The point of departure for GIS data processing is the primary parcel dataset provided by the LINZ data service (Land Information New Zealand, 2018[1]). A *primary parcel* is a polygon that represents a portion of land serving a single, observable land-use type from a set of 47 classes. The size of a primary parcel may vary widely, from a few square metres to surfaces exceeding a square kilometre. The upper left panel of Figure 4.1 displays a large number of primary parcels within and around Auckland's CBD. Several primary parcels compose a *meshblock* (upper right panel) and several meshblocks make up an *area unit* (lower left panel). Meshblocks and area units are fundamental spatial delimitations at which census information is available. Finally, the lower right panel displays the model zones used in the present study. These zones are either distinct area units, or small concatenations (groups of 2-3) of them.

Figure 4.1. The hierarchical structure of GIS information

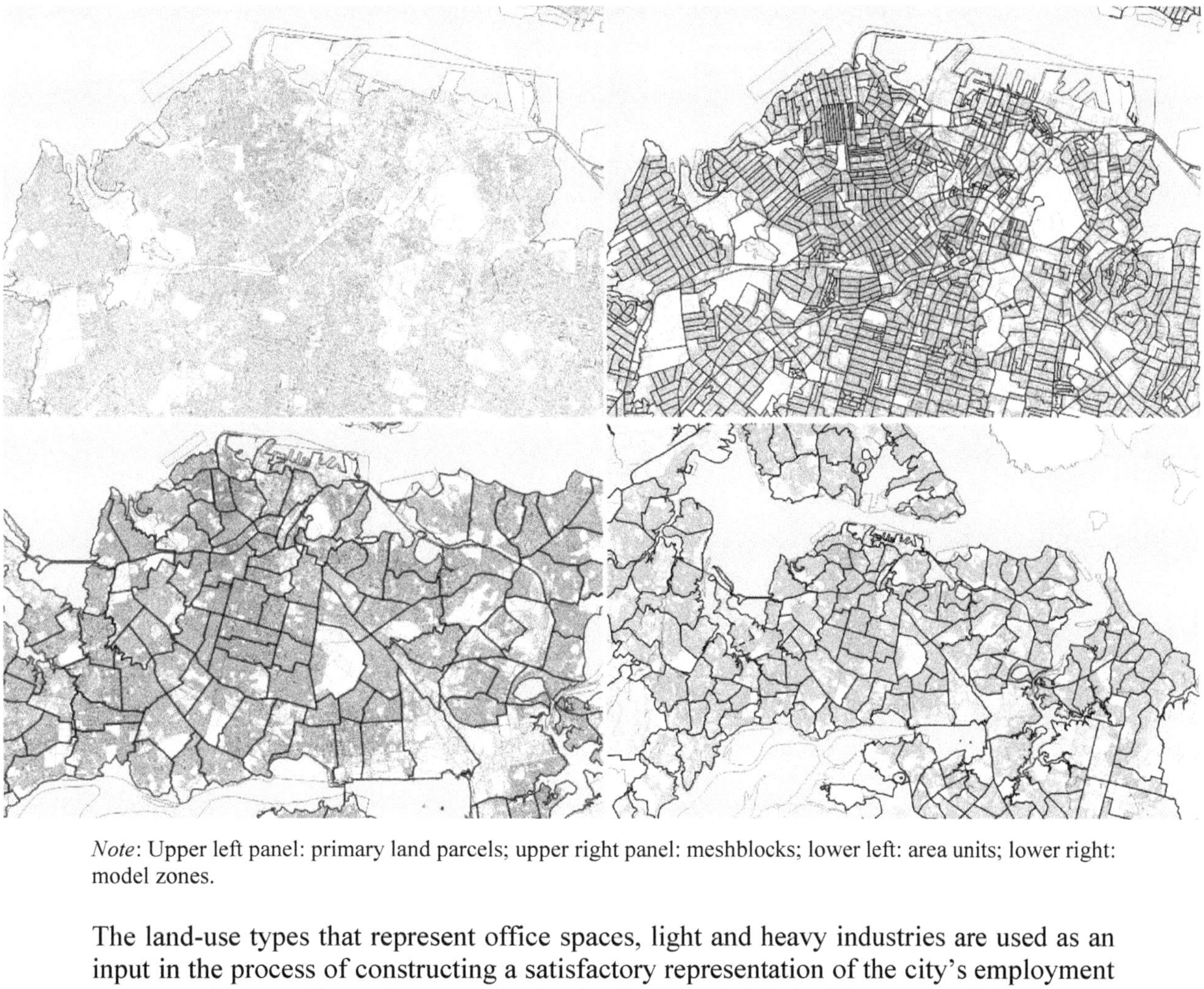

Note: Upper left panel: primary land parcels; upper right panel: meshblocks; lower left: area units; lower right: model zones.

The land-use types that represent office spaces, light and heavy industries are used as an input in the process of constructing a satisfactory representation of the city's employment patterns with a small set of commuting destinations, i.e. job hubs. The output of that process is shown in Figure 4.2.

Figure 4.2. From employment primary parcels in GIS data to job hubs in MOLES

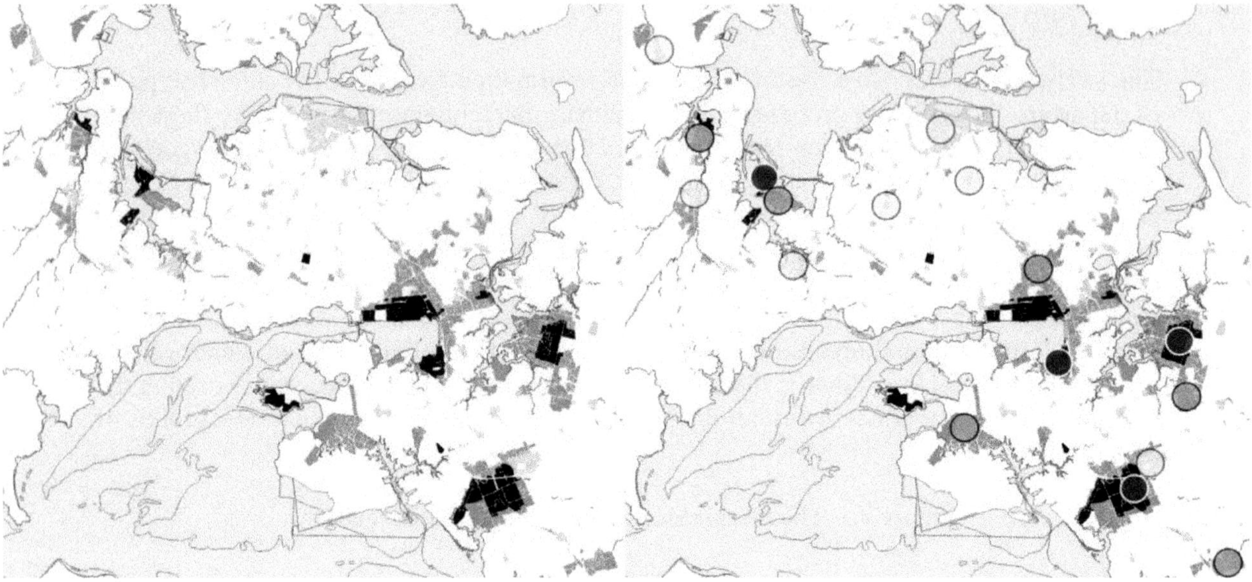

Note: Left panel: employment primary parcels; right panel: employment primary parcels and representative job hubs. Colour representation: light grey: office jobs; dark grey: light industry; black: heavy industry and quarries.

Figure 4.3. From residential primary parcels to housing locations in MOLES (year 2018)

Note: Left panel: Existing residential primary parcels and model zone delimitations; right panel: MOLES residential zones for base year (2018).

The GIS data on primary land parcels are also used in order to distinguish the model zones that contain a substantial surface of residential land. Such zones could be used as residential zones in the base year of the model simulations (2018). This extraction process is shown in Figure 4.3, where all residential parcels of land are displayed together with the model zones that contain them (left panel). The right panel of the figure shows how the various concentration levels of residential land in model zones translate to a selection of model zones in which housing and land markets will be considered. Figure 4.4 displays the same exercise for the horizon year of the study. That is done by adding the land parcels that have been reserved for future residential development. The addition of these land parcels, which are shown in brown in the left panel of the picture, expands the choice of the selected model zones acting as residential locations (right panel).

Figure 4.4. From residential primary parcels to housing locations in MOLES (year 2050)

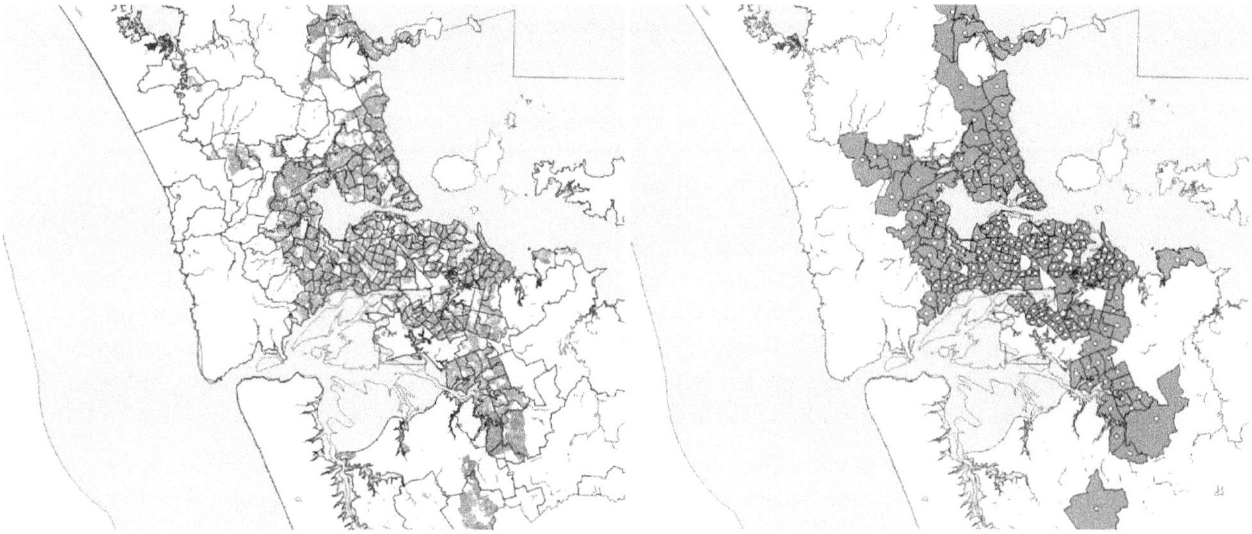

Note: Left panel: Existing (in grey), future (in brown) residential primary parcels and model zone delimitations; right panel: MOLES residential zones for the study's horizon year (2050). New residential zones appear in brown.

Apart from being used in isolation in order to identify residential and job locations, GIS data are used in combination with data from the travel survey to identify the locations of shopping hubs and the key destinations of leisure trips.

4.1.2. Travel survey data

The study uses data from an extensive household travel survey carried out between 2003 and 2014 (New Zealand Ministry of Transport, 2018[2]). That survey covers 68 000 people from 27 000 households in New Zealand and generates information that is organized in several interrelated datasets summarised in Table 4.1. The study uses also survey data from trips conducted within Auckland. The travel survey contains information on current mobility patterns by recording representative trips from households and individuals. The records include details on the origin, destination, distance and duration of trips, the transport mode used and the household status. For the purposes of the model, the Trip (TR) dataset is linked to the Addresses (AD) dataset to obtain coordinates of the origin, destination and distance of every trip contained in the dataset.

Table 4.1. Travel survey datasets

Household (HH)	Information on the household surveyed including household type and response status.
Person (PE)	Basic socioeconomic information of the respondent (age, gender, experience, occupation, income), work and school locations.
Trip (TR)	Trip characteristics (Purpose, mode, date, time, distance of each trip leg) and vehicle information.
Trip chains(CH)	Trip components (legs) composing trip chains. Two successive trip legs may be part of the same chain only if the latter is undertaken within 30 minutes from the completion of the former.
Vehicle (VE)	Characteristics of each vehicle used by the respondents of the survey including type, make, model, year and engine capacity.
Address (AD)	Address, place name, geocode of trip destinations and accuracy of geocode.

Source: (New Zealand Ministry of Transport, 2018[2]).

In the initial processing stage, the trips of the travel survey were grouped according to the time and the purpose of the journey. The classification with respect to the trip's time involved the exact same three periods that mirror the model's temporal specification: on-peak weekday travel, off-peak weekday travel and weekend travel. Trips commencing before the start of the on-peak period but ending within it, or *vice versa*, were assigned to each period proportionately to the share of the trip duration falling within each of them.

Originally, trip purpose is classified in six major categories: home-returning, commuting, education, shopping, leisure and miscellaneous (i.e. trips serving any purpose other than the five listed). Home-returning trips account for 35% of reported trips. The actual purpose of home-returning trips is identified with the help of an auxiliary method. That method matches the origin of the home-returning trip to the destination of a trip undertaken earlier by the same respondent, provided that it is possible to infer the purpose of that original trip. For instance, if a respondent reported a trip to work at some point in time and a home-returning trip in the some latter time point during the same day, the two trips are matched and recorded as commuting trips.

In several instances, matching is complicated by the fact that multiple trips of different purposes are candidates to match a home-returning trip. For instance, a respondent may report a trip to a shopping mall as a shopping trip on one occasion but a leisure trip on another occasion. If the original purpose of the home-returning trip is not clear, the study assigns an equal probability to the various matching purposes. In the context of the mentioned example, this implies that the home-returning trip from this location is recorded as being 50% a shopping trip and 50% a leisure trip.

After implementing this method, more than 96% of home-returning trips were matched and reclassified as commuting, education, shopping, leisure or miscellaneous trips. Using these data manipulations results in the temporal and modal decomposition of passenger kilometres reported in Table 4.2 and Table 4.3 respectively.

Table 4.2. Modal and temporal split of passenger kilometres for each trip purpose

Period	Mode	Work	Education	Shopping	Leisure	Other
On-peak	All	55.32%	60.39%	21.46%	24.89%	32.48%
	0=Pedestrian	0.62%	5.48%	0.62%	0.95%	0.56%
	1='Car'/ van driver	44.65%	13.28%	14.58%	14.68%	19.58%
	2='Car'/van passenger	4.13%	26.45%	4.76%	8.39%	11.23%
	3=Cyclist	0.22%	0.22%	0.07%	0.21%	0.02%
	5='Local' PT (bus/train/ferry)*	3.27%	14.18%	1.25%	0.42%	0.61%
	9='Other' household travel	0.17%	0.14%	0.03%	0.08%	0.06%
	10=Motorcyclist	0.40%	0.05%	0.03%	0.10%	0.06%
	11='Non-household' travel (trucks, tractors, taxi driver etc.)	1.86%	0.58%	0.13%	0.07%	0.37%
	20='Non-local' PT*	0.00%	0.00%	0.00%	0.00%	0.00%
Off-peak	All	35.82%	34.23%	38.31%	29.68%	38.51%
	0=Pedestrian	0.35%	3.89%	1.08%	0.98%	0.72%
	1='Car'/ van driver	30.26%	10.06%	26.78%	18.52%	21.41%
	2='Car'/van passenger	2.35%	10.76%	8.68%	8.96%	14.92%
	3=Cyclist	0.11%	0.30%	0.03%	0.22%	0.01%
	5='Local' PT (bus/train/ferry)*	0.76%	8.45%	1.37%	0.75%	0.70%
	9='Other' household travel	0.11%	0.35%	0.10%	0.10%	0.07%
	10=Motorcyclist	0.22%	0.04%	0.06%	0.09%	0.06%
	11='Non-household' travel (trucks, tractors, taxi driver etc.)	1.56%	0.39%	0.21%	0.05%	0.37%
	20='Non-local' PT*	0.10%	0.00%	0.00%	0.00%	0.25%
Weekend	All	8.85%	5.38%	40.23%	45.42%	29.00%
	0=Pedestrian	0.06%	0.17%	0.67%	0.84%	0.18%
	1='Car'/ van driver	7.29%	2.15%	25.01%	22.55%	13.11%
	2='Car'/van passenger	0.92%	2.43%	14.08%	20.50%	15.32%
	3=Cyclist	0.02%	0.00%	0.02%	0.49%	0.01%
	5='Local' PT (bus/train/ferry)*	0.27%	0.64%	0.32%	0.47%	0.20%
	9='Other' household travel	0.01%	0.00%	0.00%	0.37%	0.12%
	10=Motorcyclist	0.05%	0.00%	0.04%	0.07%	0.00%
	11='Non-household' travel (trucks, tractors, taxi driver etc.)	0.23%	0.00%	0.09%	0.14%	0.06%
	20='Non-local' PT*	0.00%	0.00%	0.00%	0.00%	0.00%

Source: (New Zealand Ministry of Transport, 2018[2]).

Table 4.3. Purpose split of passenger kilometres for each mode and time period.

Period	Mode	Work	Education	Shop	Leisure	Other
On-peak	All	46.08%	8.84%	7.34%	16.37%	20.31%
	0=Pedestrian	20.52%	32.03%	8.41%	25.01%	14.02%
	1='Car'/ van driver	56.34%	2.94%	7.55%	14.62%	18.55%
	2='Car'/van passenger	16.03%	18.02%	7.59%	25.69%	32.67%
	3=Cyclist	47.58%	8.36%	5.83%	35.55%	2.69%
	5='Local' PT (bus/train/ferry)*	46.30%	35.32%	7.24%	4.69%	6.44%
	9='Other' household travel	54.55%	7.87%	4.11%	19.85%	13.62%
	10=Motorcyclist	73.14%	1.65%	2.58%	13.86%	8.77%
	11='Non-household' travel (trucks, tractors, taxi driver etc.)	79.27%	4.35%	2.19%	2.37%	11.82%
	20='Non-local' PT*	0.00%	0.00%	0.00%	0.00%	0.00%
Off-peak	All	32.59%	5.47%	14.31%	21.32%	26.30%
	0=Pedestrian	12.61%	24.42%	15.90%	27.63%	19.44%
	1='Car'/ van driver	41.05%	2.40%	14.92%	19.83%	21.80%
	2='Car'/van passenger	9.02%	7.25%	13.67%	27.13%	42.94%
	3=Cyclist	30.34%	14.99%	3.70%	48.68%	2.29%
	5='Local' PT (bus/train/ferry)*	19.27%	37.85%	14.39%	15.09%	13.41%
	9='Other' household travel	31.61%	17.75%	11.48%	23.56%	15.61%
	10=Motorcyclist	59.97%	1.69%	6.51%	20.07%	11.75%
	11='Non-household' travel (trucks, tractors, taxi driver etc.)	76.80%	3.34%	4.20%	2.12%	13.54%
	20='Non-local' PT*	34.77%	0.00%	0.00%	0.00%	65.23%
Weekend	All	10.54%	1.13%	19.68%	42.72%	25.93%
	0=Pedestrian	5.27%	2.52%	23.75%	57.03%	11.43%
	1='Car'/ van driver	15.99%	0.83%	22.53%	39.06%	21.59%
	2='Car'/van passenger	2.65%	1.23%	16.61%	46.48%	33.03%
	3=Cyclist	4.71%	0.00%	1.77%	91.54%	1.98%
	5='Local' PT (bus/train/ferry)*	26.16%	10.83%	12.76%	35.75%	14.50%
	9='Other' household travel	2.05%	0.00%	0.13%	74.30%	23.52%
	10=Motorcyclist	43.47%	0.00%	12.71%	43.82%	0.00%
	11='Non-household' travel (trucks, tractors, taxi driver etc.)	53.60%	0.00%	8.30%	26.93%	11.16%
	20='Non-local' PT*	0.00%	0.00%	0.00%	0.00%	0.00%

Source: (New Zealand Ministry of Transport, 2018[2]).

Subsequently, the commuting trips from the travel survey are geolocated (i.e. mapped) and used in combination with the GIS data. That yields a measure of the labour force's share that is employed in each of the employment hubs. That exercise is displayed in Figure 4.5, where the destination points of the commuting trips are geolocated. The buffer zones surrounding the various employment hubs adjust in order to minimise: (i) the number of trips not being captured by any employment hub and (ii) the overlap between job hub domains of the same type (offices, light and heavy industries). This heuristic method results in a large portion of the commuting trip destination points (82%) falling within the constructed buffer zones. Many of the commuting trips the method fails to capture terminate in rural locations, reserved for agriculture. This indicates that these trips are likely to represent respondents commuting to jobs in the agricultural sector. As the agricultural sector is not modelled explicitly, these data are not used in the analysis that follows.

Figure 4.5. Using the travel survey to approximate the share of job hubs in total employment

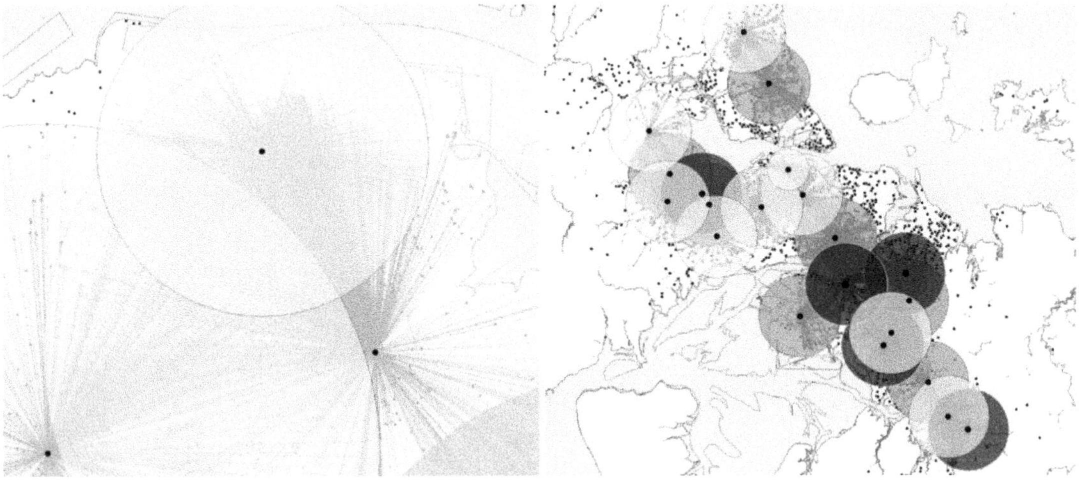

Note: Left panel: distance-based allocation of trips that terminate in overlapping employment hub domains; Right panel: overlapping domains of neighbouring employment hubs.

Due to the proximity of employment hubs of different types (e.g. a light industry hub may lie in the proximity of a heavy industry hub), a substantial overlap of two or more job hub domains is in many cases inevitable. That holds true especially in the area of the isthmus, where hubs are located close to each other. That area is displayed in the right panel of Figure 4.5. A drawback of the travel survey is that the employment type of the commuter cannot be inferred by the incorporated information. This implies that a trip destination point that belongs to the multiple buffer zones cannot be assigned with certainty to any of them. This is true even if the overlapping areas represent the domains of very different job concentrations, for example office jobs and heavy industries. To overcome this obstacle, the study uses a probabilistic method to assign a weight to each candidate job hub of a commuting trip. That weight is inversely related to the distance between the work trip destination and the employment hub. That is, the closer a job hub lies to the terminal point of a trip, the more likely it is to be the actual destination of the commuter and *vice versa*. Using the same weighting method, self-reported income data are linked to employment hubs in order to approximate the mean income of an employee at each employment hub.

Figure 4.6. Using the travel survey to map shopping hubs.

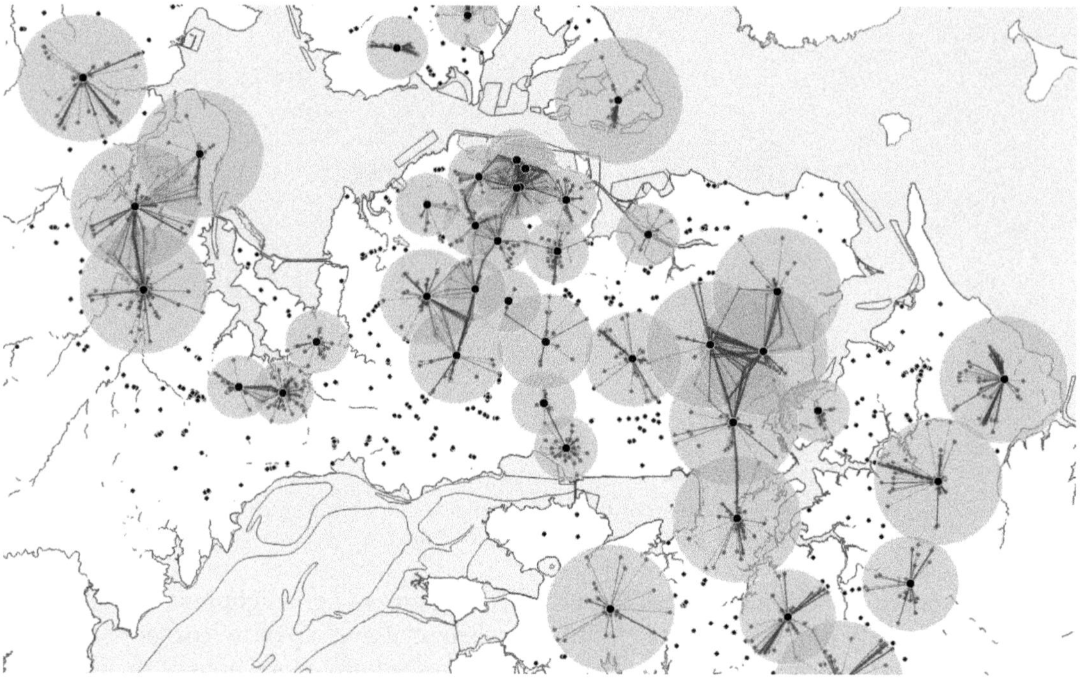

Note: Small black dots display the destination points of shopping trips; large black dots display shopping hubs and the grey circles around them display the impact territory (buffer zone) of a hub.

The study uses the same methodology to map shopping trips to shopping hubs. Shopping hubs are created in areas where primary land parcels of mixed use are highly concentrated. They are also directly geolocated in the case of large shopping centres. Buffer zones of various sizes are created to capture, within their domains, a satisfactory share (93.7%) of the shopping trip destinations, as shown in Figure 4.6. The same distance-weighting formula that is used to allocate commuting trips to multiple employment hubs is used to assign shopping trips to multiple candidate shopping hubs. That is, whenever the destination point of a shopping trip lies within the domain of multiple such shopping hubs, the relative proximity of that point to each hub determines the degree to which the former belongs to the latter.

Unlike the destination points of commuting and shopping trips, which display a clear spatial pattern, the respective destination points of leisure trips are scattered in a uniform manner across the entire urban fabric, as shown in the left panel of Figure 4.7. To represent leisure locations in a convenient manner, the study uses 26 points that are scattered uniformly across urban space. A fixed impact territory, i.e. buffer zone, of a three kilometre radius around these points is sufficient to capture 90.1% of leisure trip destinations.

Figure 4.7. Using the travel survey to map locations of leisure hubs.

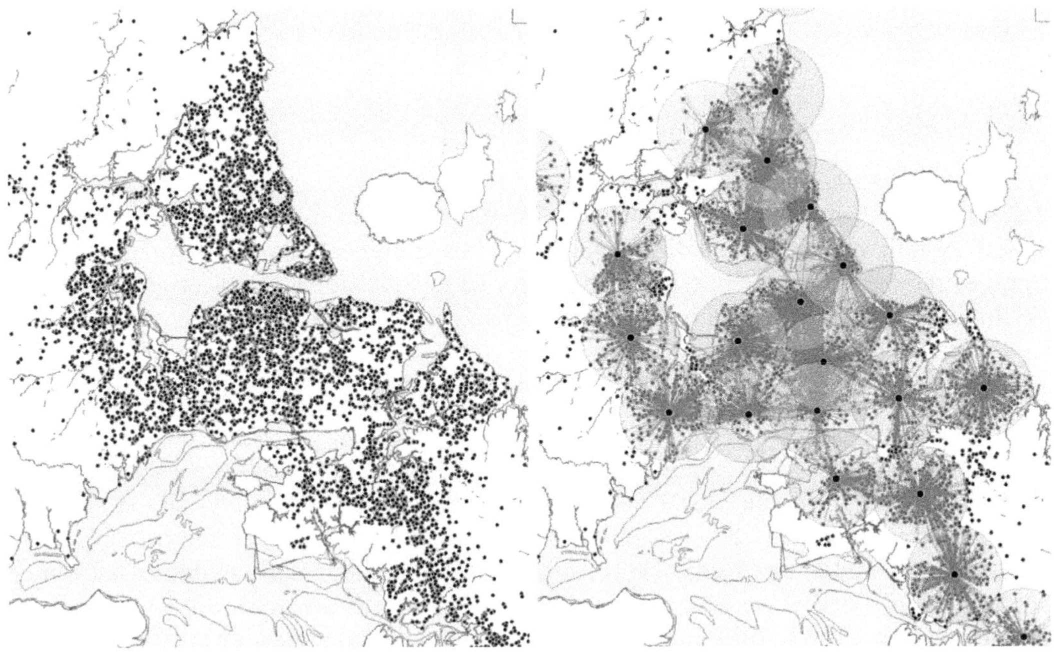

Note: Small black dots display the destination points of leisure trips; large black dots display shopping hubs and the grey circles around them display the impact territory of hub.

Schooling trips are omitted from the analysis, as their contribution to the total amount of emissions is too small to justify the use of the computer-intensive methods deployed to model commuting, shopping and leisure trips. More specifically, schooling trips taken with private cars (the most carbon-intensive transport mode) make up between 1.4% and 3.6% of the total kilometres driven.[1] To provide a sense of proportions, the share of commuting trips, shopping and leisure trips in total kilometres is 28.3%, 12.2% and 23.4% respectively.

4.1.3. Fuel efficiency

The average *fuel economy* of the New Zealand's future fleet of conventional vehicles is among the important determinants of the study's outcomes.[2] Vehicle fuel economy is expressed as the number of kilometres driven with one litre of gasoline. Since the evolution of that variable up to 2050 is unknown, it is projected using the evolution of fuel efficiency in a sample of the Auckland's conventional fleet from 1994 to 2018 (New Zealand Transport Agency, 2018[3]).

The evolution of the observed fuel efficiency is decomposed into a *time trend* and a *vehicle build* trend. The time trend encapsulates the overall technological progress in the automobile industry. It implies that a vehicle produced today is more fuel-efficient than a vehicle with the same observable characteristics produced in the past. The vehicle build trend implies that the average vehicle produced today has a different fuel efficiency than a vehicle produced in the past because vehicle attributes that determine fuel efficiency evolve over time. These attributes include the body type, weight, the engine type (conventional or hybrid) and capacity of the average vehicle in the fleet, as well as the market shares of the various manufacturers. The vehicle build trend captures the part of the of fuel efficiency variation that can be attributed to the fact that vehicles in a given point in time are heterogeneous: they are produced by different manufactures, weigh different amounts, have differing engine capacities and are operated in different ways. Due to this heterogeneity, vehicles produced in the same year are likely to exhibit different levels of fuel efficiency. The time trend, as well as the different trends in vehicle build extracted from the evolution of vehicle attributes, are used to extrapolate the observed fuel efficiency to the period between 2018 and 2050. The projection is based on the assumption that the multiple determinants of fuel economy will continue evolving along their in-sample trajectories.

One important driver of fuel economy evolution is the increase in the share of hybrid vehicles in the fleet. That is because hybrid vehicles are, on average, significantly more fuel-efficient than gasoline and diesel vehicles. Thus, a higher share of hybrids in the fleet improves the overall fuel economy of the fleet. To account for this aspect, the projection accounts explicitly for their share in the future fleet. More specific, it assumes that the latter share will evolve according to the current trend.

4.1.4. Other data

The model generates traffic conditions and vehicle speeds that vary across the three time intervals (on-peak, off-peak, weekends) composing a week. They also vary spatially, across the cells of the 1.8 km × 1.8 km grid and across the different highway segments. In order to calibrate the model parameters that relate the levels of traffic (traffic volumes) to vehicle speeds, observations on the latter are needed. Vehicle speeds are observed with the use of Google Distance Matrix API. This database service uses accumulated observations of travel speeds and their determinants, such as day, time, season, mode of transport, and weather conditions, to predict travel time between any pair of locations.

Figure 4.8. Grid cells and grid cell groups at which speed is measured

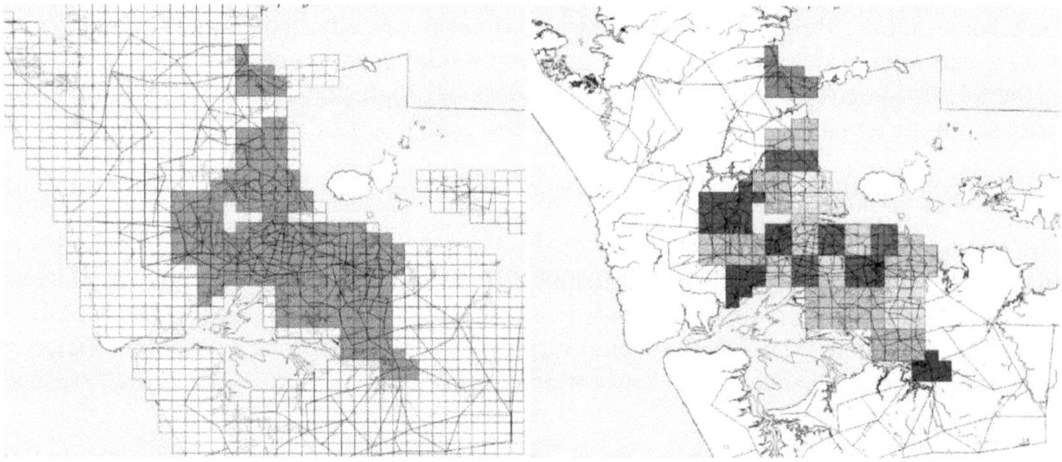

Note: Left panel: the shaded part of the grid represents areas where the speeds are predicted by the model; the non-shaded part represents areas where speed is exogenous. Right panel: the 22 cell groups from which speed observations are drawn using the Google API.

Observations on vehicle speeds across the various grid cells are drawn separately for each of the three representative time intervals (on-peak, off-peak and weekends). The speed data collection is performed separately for privately-owned and public transport vehicles. The underlying road network is sparse in a large portion of the grid, which is represented by the set of non-coloured cells in the left panel of Figure 4.8. These are predominantly rural areas, in which the average traffic flows are low and the average speeds lie close to their free-flow levels, independent of the time of the day or the day of the week. To simplify matters,

MOLES sets the speeds within those cells equal to their free-flow levels. In turn, the free-flow speeds are approximated with observations drawn from selected parts of the non-coloured part of the grid in Figure 4.8. Once these speeds are set in line with data, MOLES treats them as exogenous.

In the rest of the grid, time-averaged traffic flows are considerable and fluctuate both across cells and across the three time intervals. A large number of observations is drawn from the coloured part of the grid in Figure 4.8 to approximate the vehicle speeds with spatiotemporal accuracy. However, there is an upper bound on the distance between any pair of points within a single 1.8 km × 1.8 km grid cell, which lies slightly below 2.55 km. That ceiling value sets an upper bound on the distance and travel time of the trips that are sampled to calculate the average speed in the cell. This implies that the latter is systematically underestimated, as the underlying calculations include fixed time requirements for parking or (in the case of public transport) transit. To reduce that bias, the cells are grouped into 22 groups, which are displayed in the right panel of Figure 4.8. The grouping takes into account the homogeneity of network and aims at generating well-shaped cell groups that would contain the straight-line connections between the origin and destination points drawn within them.

Figure 4.9. The highway network and the highway link groups at which speed is measured

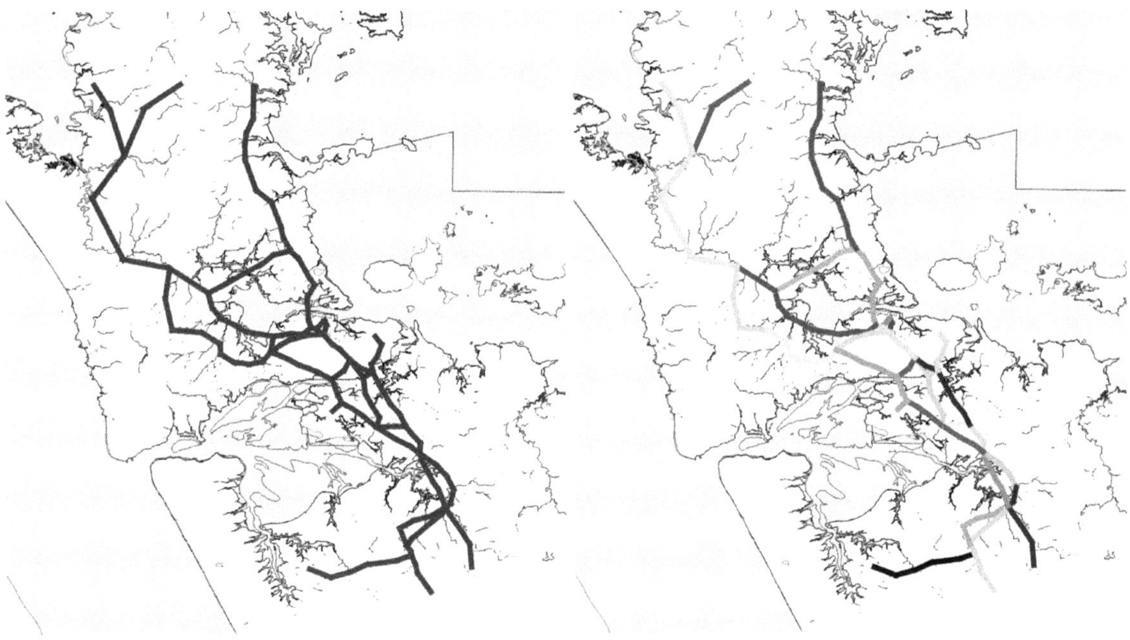

Note: Left panel: the highway network, as represented in MOLES. Right panel: the 26 link groups from which speed observations are drawn using the Google API.

A similar method is used to group adjacent links in the highway network representation. The grouping of highway links is shown in the left panel of Figure 4.9.

4.2. Model calibration

4.2.1. Population and employment densities

The model is calibrated in order to reproduce a series of stylised facts that characterise New Zealand and to be aligned with general empirical regularities reported in the literature. Regarding the variables determined at the local level, the model's outcomes accord with the data processed specifically for the urban area of Auckland. The benchmark equilibrium approximates the observed population density in each model zone (left panel of Figure 4.10) and the employment density in each job hub (right panel of Figure 4.10).[3]

Figure 4.10. Population and employment densities reproduced in the benchmark equilibrium

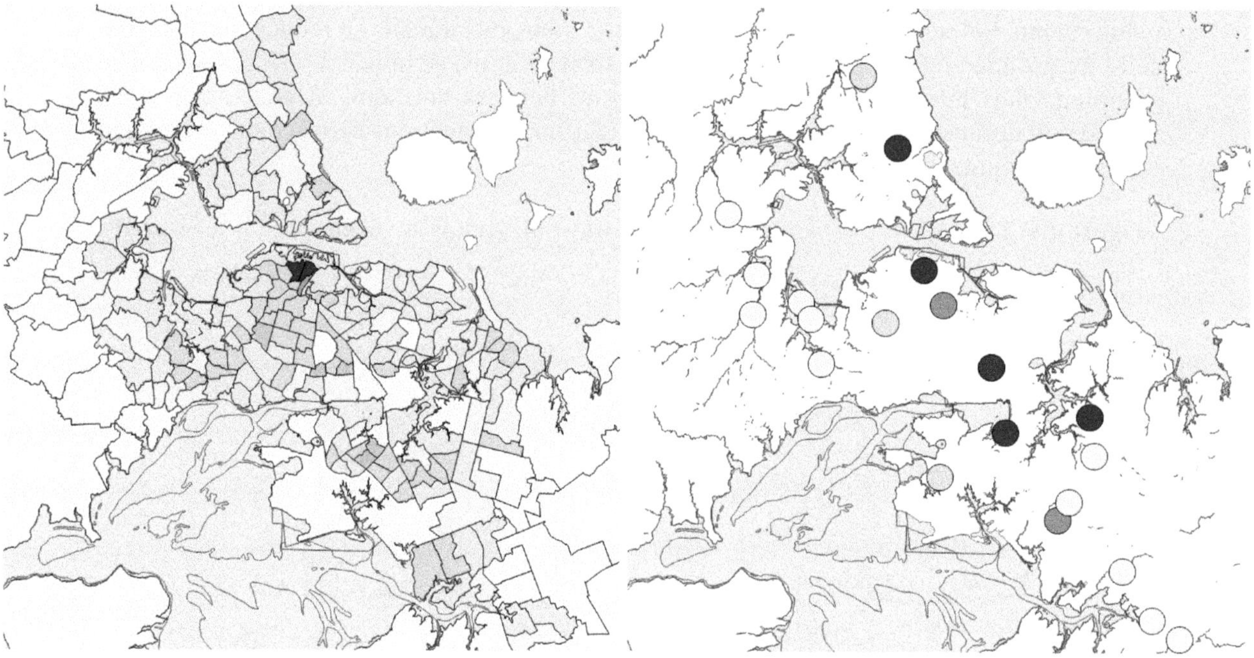

Note: Left panel: population density by model zone; right panel: employment density by job hub. Darker colours indicate higher population and employment densities.

Table 4.4. Benchmark equilibrium values

Expenditure share of income	
Consumption	0.639
Housing expenditure	0.260
Transport expenditure	0.101
Income share by source	
Labour remuneration	0.767
Rents	0.233
Value of time	
Average value of time weekdays (NZD/hour)	13.80
Average value of time weekends (NZD/hour)	4.43
Key elasticities [a]	
Own-price elasticity of housing demand	-0.614
Income elasticity of housing demand	1.00
Income elasticity of consumption	1.00
Private vehicle ownership rate (%)	
Internal combustion engine [c]	89.4%
Electric vehicle	0.6%
Modal split in commuting trips (%)	
Car	77.4 %
Public transport	13.3 %
Soft mobility [b]	9.3 %
Modal split in shopping trips	
Car	86.9 %
Soft mobility [b]	13.1 %
Modal split in leisure trips	
Car	78.1 %
Public transport	1.1%
Soft mobility [b]	20.8%
Temporal split in shopping detours	
Probability of making a shopping detour on a week day	0.514
Conditional probability of making the detour during on-peak	0.44
Conditional probability of making the detour trip during off-peak	0.56
Probability of making a shopping detour on a weekend day	0.114
Temporal split in home-based shopping trips	
Probability of making a shopping trip on a week day	0.290
Conditional probability of making the shopping trip during on-peak	0.04
Conditional probability of making the shopping trip during off-peak	0.96
Probability of making a shopping trip on a weekend day	0.477
Temporal split in home-based leisure trips	
Probability of making a leisure trip on a week day	0.280
Conditional probability of making the leisure trip during on-peak	0.0
Conditional probability of making the leisure trip during off-peak	1.0
Probability of making a leisure trip on a weekend day	0.508

Note: [a] Represent probability-weighted means of the corresponding elasticities computed conditional on the choice of each alternative. Future versions will provide additional elasticity measures. [b] Includes walking and biking. [c] Includes diesel and hybrid cars.
Source: Model output.

4.2.2. Income and value of time distributions

On average, 64% of the disposable income in the model is spent on consumption goods, 26% on housing and 10% on transport. These average numbers are in rough alignment with overall estimates generated by processing data from the Census. The distributions of the three expenditure shares, as predicted by the model, are displayed in Figure 4.11. Two main drivers underlie the variation in expenditure patterns predicted by the model. The first one is the spatial trade-off between transport and housing costs. That is, housing costs are higher in the most accessible locations, as jobs, shopping and leisure hubs can be reached with a relatively low pecuniary and time cost from these locations. Therefore, some individuals face relatively high housing costs and low transport costs, and *vice versa*. This mechanism accords with general empirical regularities and is in alignment with information obtained specifically for Auckland from a household expenditure survey. The second driver is the possibility of substitution between generic consumption and the rest of expenditure sources. For instance, individuals with high valuations of residential space will have to decrease their consumption levels in order to finance the larger housing costs they face.

Figure 4.11. Expenditure shares of income

The distribution of the share of income spent on consumption, housing and transport across households

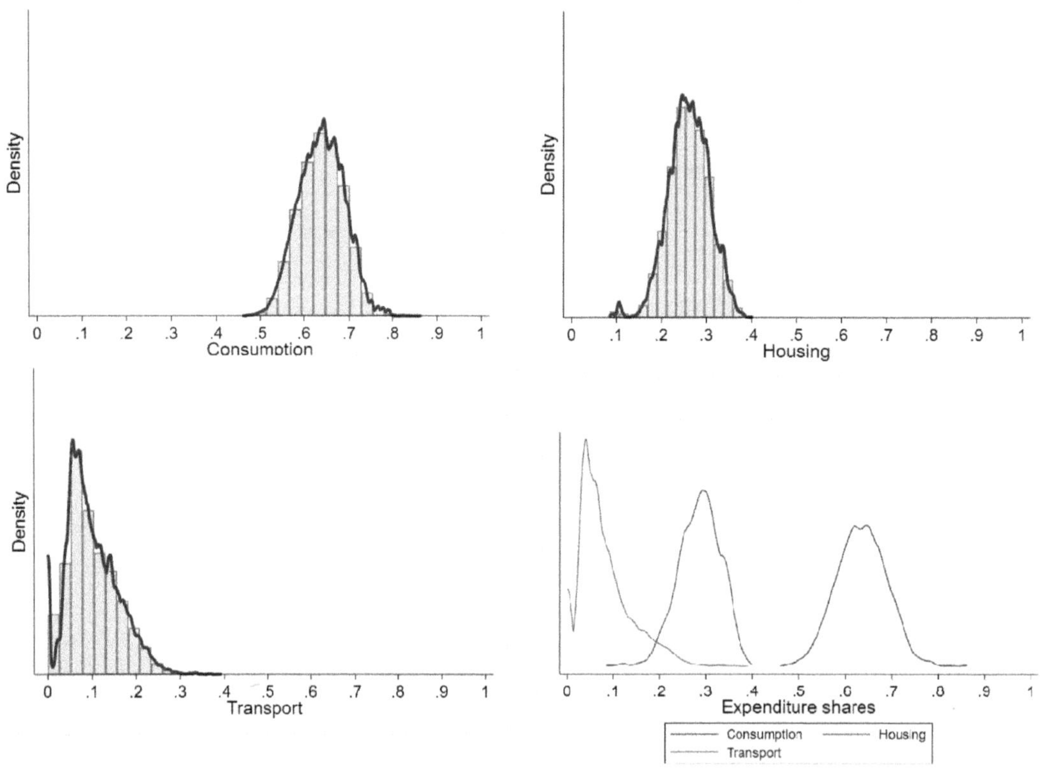

Source: Generated by the authors.

Labour remuneration accounts for approximately 77% of the income generated in the simulations. The respective share of rents is 23%. The resulting net expenditure on housing is in accordance with rough estimates derived from processing the census data.

The mean value of time during a weekday is NZD 13.80 per hour. During weekends, that value falls to NZD 4.43 per hour. Both these means lie within the range of values proposed in the literature (ITF, 2017[4]). The underlying distributions of time valuation during working and non-working days are displayed in Figure 4.12. The average price elasticity of housing demand, which indicates the rigidity of residential space demand with respect to changes in housing prices, is -0.61. The associated income elasticities of housing and consumption are both unitary.[4]

Figure 4.12. Value of time distributions

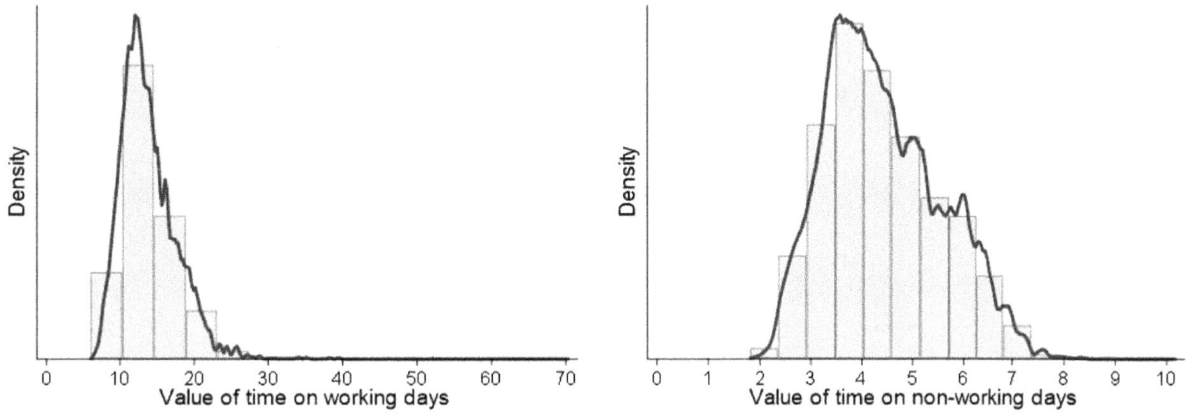

Source: Generated by the authors.

The benchmark equilibrium yields an ownership rate (90%) that approximates the observed one. The shares of conventional and electric vehicles in the model, 99.4% and 0.6% respectively, lie close to the ones estimated from data (99.7% and 0.3%).

The travel behaviour predicted by the model fits the observations of the travel survey. That is, 77.4% of commuters use a private vehicle (85.1% in data), 13.3% use public transport (8.5% in data) and 9.3% of commuting takes place with soft mobility (6.4% in data).[5]

On average, an individual has a probability of 29% to make a home-based shopping trip during a weekday. If that home-based trip is realised, it most probably (96%) takes place during the off-peak hours. Home-based shopping trips occur with high probability (47.7%) during a typical weekend day. Furthermore, shopping detours can be incorporated into commuting trips. This occurs with a probability that exceeds 50% for commuting trips in weekdays and falls to 11% for the commuting trips occurring in weekend days. The vast majority of these shopping trips, 86.9%, are undertaken with a private vehicle, while a smaller portion, 13.1%, uses soft mobility. The corresponding estimates from the travel survey data are 86.5% and 13.5% respectively.

4.2.3. Vehicle speeds

Figure 4.13. Speeds of private vehicles driving on the road network across different time periods

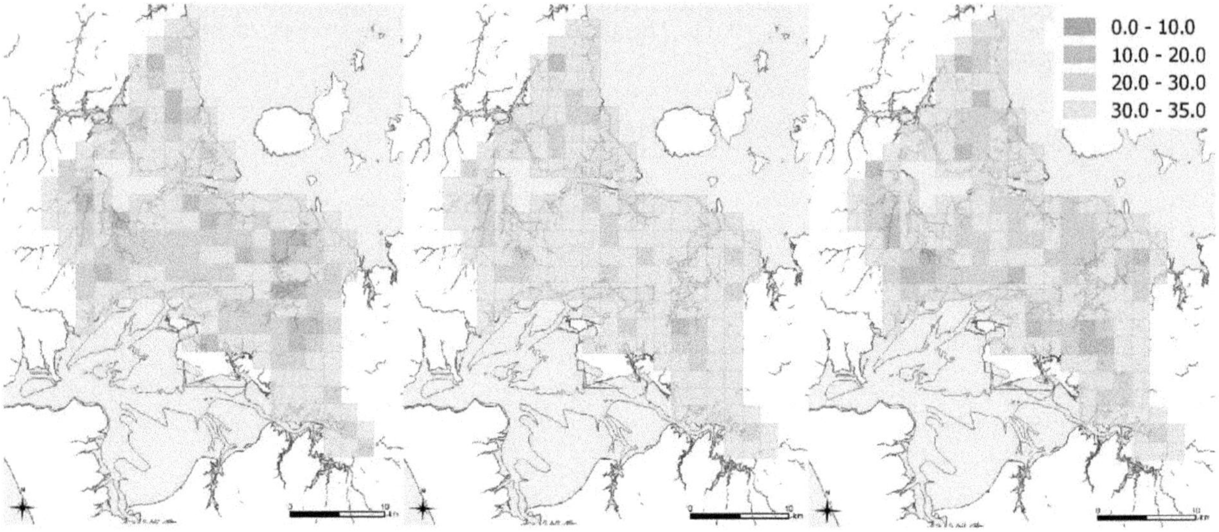

Note: Left panel: speeds at peak periods during weekdays; central panel: speeds at off-peak periods during weekdays; right panel; speeds during weekends. Maximum speed on the road network for private vehicles is 50 km/h. All speeds are in km/h.

Private vehicle travel speeds produced by the model were highest during off-peak periods (central panel in Figure 4.13) where vehicle speeds across the grid approached the maximum vehicle speed of 35 kilometres/hour. As expected, speeds are at their lowest level during peak periods (left panel in Figure 4.13). In those periods, the average travel speed lies between 10 and 20 kilometres per hour in areas of the network connecting the residential zones with the Central Business District (CBD). A substantial number of shopping and leisure trips taking place on weekends contribute to reduced speeds in many areas of the network (right panel in Figure 4.13).

Figure 4.14. Speeds of public buses

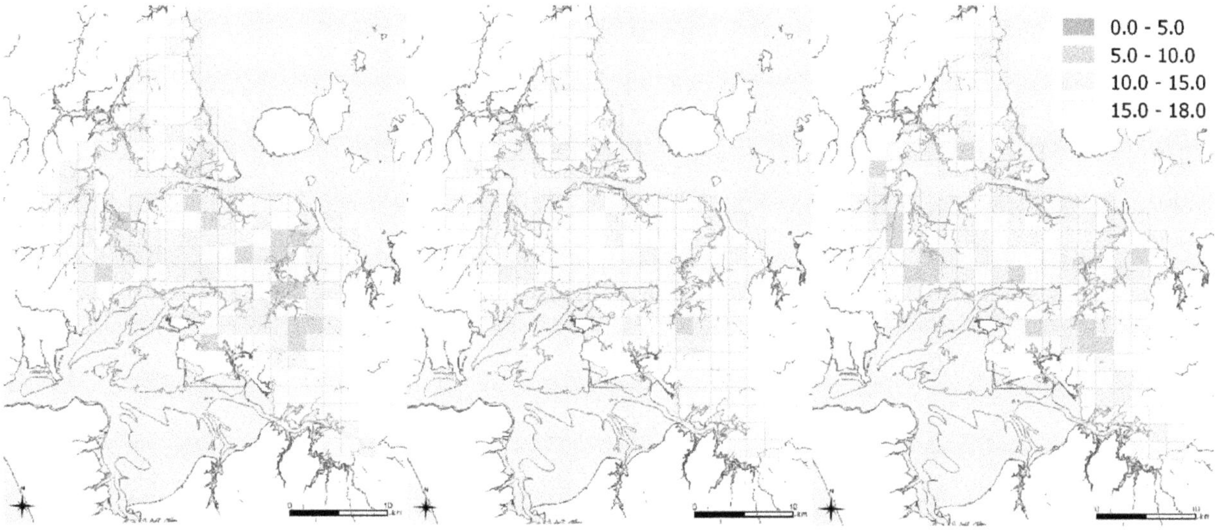

Note: Left panel: speeds at peak periods during weekdays; central panel: speeds at off-peak periods during weekdays; right panel; speeds during weekends. Maximum speed on the public transport network is 30 km/h. All speeds in km/h.

Travelling with public transport in Auckland implies, to a large extent, the use of public buses. These use fixed routes, most of the times in the same road segments used by private cars, and make frequent stops. Therefore, the model assumes a low free-flow speed for buses (17 km/h). In many areas of the network, speed falls short of 10 kilometres per hour during the peak traffic hours on weekdays (left panel in Figure 4.14). Travel speeds are relatively higher in off-peak periods (central panel in Figure 4.14) and on weekends (left panel in Figure 4.14) but remain low in the busiest areas of the network.

Figure 4.15. Speeds of private vehicles on the highway network

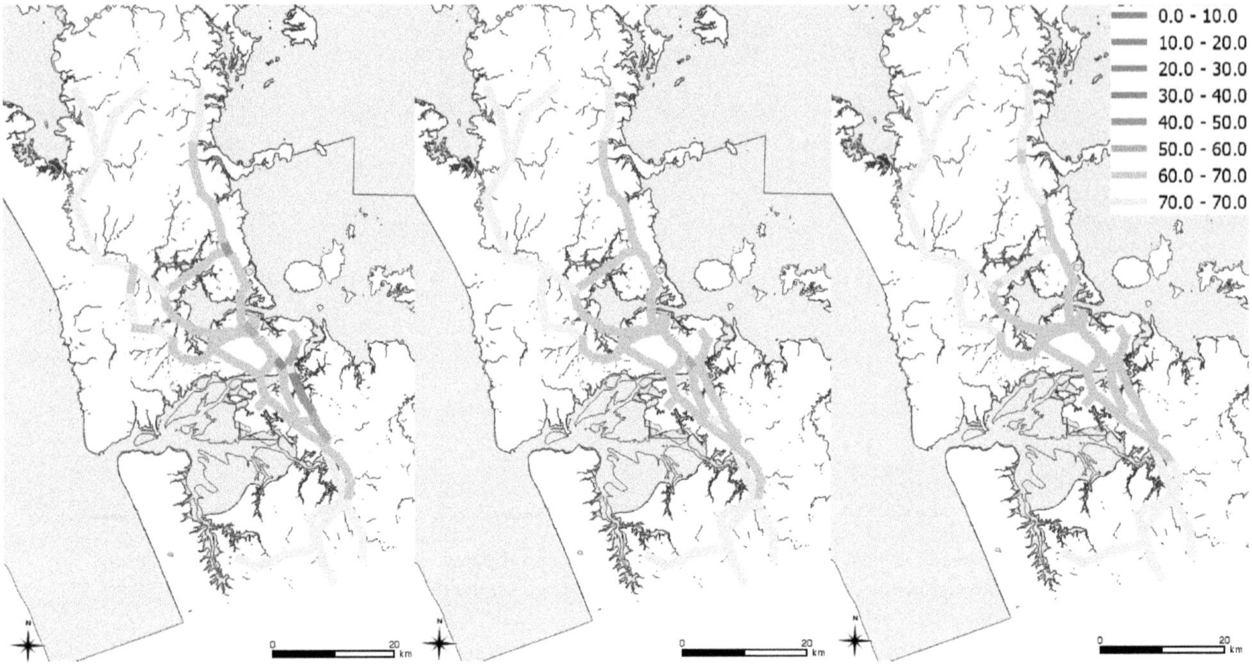

Note: Left panel: speeds at peak periods during weekdays; central panel: speeds at off-peak periods during weekdays; right panel; speeds during weekends. Maximum speed on the highway network is 70 km/h. All speeds in km/h.

Average speeds of private vehicles on Auckland's highway network is generally high. In many areas, speeds approach the maximum speed (i.e. the free-flow speed). That is set to of 70 km/h to account for traffic lights and any other impediment that induces a "start-stop" type of driving, even in the absence of traffic. On certain highway segments within and around the CBD, speeds fall during peak hours (left panel of Figure 4.15). In peripheral areas, speeds are close to free-flow levels during the off-peak periods of weekdays and on weekends. However, average speeds during off-peak and on weekends slow within the CBD and on highway segments leading to it from the south (central and right panel of Figure 4.15).

Notes

[1] The exact number cannot be computed with certainty due to limited information on the share of trips taken by school buses in the travel survey.

[2] Conventional cars in the study include light duty passenger cars with internal combustion or hybrid engines. The empirical work is carried out on a sample of gasoline and hybrid cars. Data on diesel cars were not of sufficient quality to be included in the econometric analysis. Instead, the evolution of the fuel economy of diesel cars is assumed to follow the trajectory as gasoline and hybrid cars do.

[3] The average difference between of the predicted shares (population in each zone, employment in each hub) and their observed counterparts is negligible, i.e. 4.9×10^{-7} and -6.1×10^{-4} respectively. The corresponding standard deviations are 3.8×10^{-4} and 1.4×10^{-3}. The observed share of each model zone in the total population is computed by summing the population of all Auckland's area units composing a model zone (see Figure 4.10). In turn, area unit populations were retrieved from the census. The actual employment density that corresponds to each job hub is approximated with probabilistic geospatial methods, which are described in Section 4.1.

[4] This is an artefact of the model specification, which assumes a constant elasticity of substitution between consumption and housing.

[5] The effect of policies on soft mobility is not analysed as the latter does not produce emissions and has zero private pecuniary costs.

References

ITF (2017), "Shared Mobility Simulations for Auckland", *International Transport Forum Policy Papers*, No. 41, OECD Publishing, Paris, https://dx.doi.org/10.1787/5423af87-en. [4]

Land Information New Zealand (2018), *LINZ data*, https://www.linz.govt.nz/data/linz-data. [1]

New Zealand Ministry of Transport (2018), *Household Travel Survey*. [2]

New Zealand Transport Agency (2018), *New Zealand vehicle fleet open data sets*, https://www.nzta.govt.nz/resources/new-zealand-motor-vehicle-register-statistics/new-zealand-vehicle-fleet-open-data-sets/. [3]

Part II.

Pathways to decarbonising urban mobility

Chapter 5. Environmental and economic implications of policy scenarios aimed at decarbonising urban transport

This chapter presents an evaluation of reference and counterfactual scenarios. The findings indicate that policy inaction can prevent urban transport from becoming carbon neutral any time soon. Under the reference scenario, in which no substantial policy change occurs, total emissions from road transport will continue increasing, while 60% of the per capita emissions in 2018 will be produced in 2050. Stringent policies that promote public transport and electric vehicles, as well as interventions that give rise to a more compact urban form may reduce the latter figure to 30%. The analysis highlights the policies that curb greenhouse gas emissions and increase welfare, while also identifying the order at which these policies should be implemented.

This chapter presents an evaluation of reference and counterfactual scenarios, as detailed in Chapter 2. The associated policy simulations are carried out with the use of MOLES (Tikoudis and Oueslati, 2017[1]). The model has been adapted for the specific needs of this case study as described in Chapter 3. It has been calibrated as described in Chapter 4. This chapter is structured across three sections. The first presents the headline results regarding emissions and vehicle use. The second offers a detailed analysis of the changes projected in the reference scenario. The third summarises the components of the policy scenario, describing the environmental, housing, fiscal and welfare implications of the different policy scenarios. Chapter 6 tests the importance of exogenous variables in driving the overall results and examines how the effectiveness of policies varies under different scenarios of demographic, socio-economic and technological change.

5.1. Headline results for greenhouse gas emissions and vehicle use

Total annual CO_2e emissions from road transport in Auckland are projected to increase by 7% in 2050, relative to emissions in year 2018. That increase is largely driven by the rise in total passenger kilometres, which are set to increase mainly due to the growing population. Thus, the effect of population growth outweighs the effect of the emission reductions stemming from various factors. These include the increasing vehicle energy efficiency, the declining costs of electric vehicle use, a less carbon-intensive electricity generation sector and the electrification of public transport.

In *per capita* terms, passenger kilometres do not change significantly between 2018 and 2050. As the carbon intensity of each transport mode falls and the share of ICE vehicles in the fleet declines, *per capita* emissions from urban transport fall across all scenarios. Transport modes become less emissions-intensive, since they consume less fuel and electricity. For EVs, emission intensity decreases also due to the further decarbonisation of the electricity grid. Additionally, the share of EVs in the fleet increases. The same holds true for the share of vehicle kilometres travelled by EVs. These increases occur because technological progress gradually increases the degree of parity between ICE vehicles and EVs. The evolution of passenger kilometres, both in total and *per capita* terms, is presented in Figure 5.1.

Figure 5.1. Evolution of total and *per capita* passenger kilometres by mode in the reference scenario

Percentage values are relative to total passenger kilometres in 2018, the base year of the study.

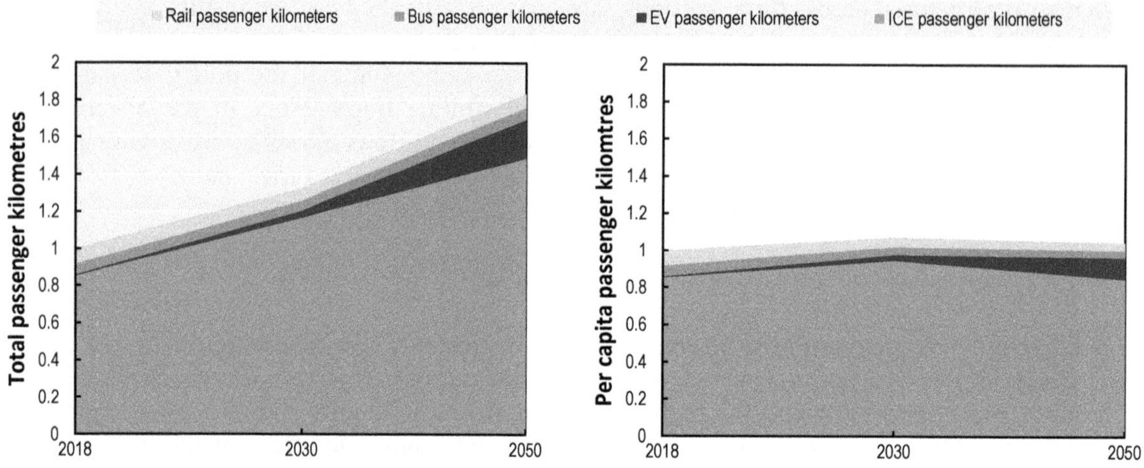

Note: Percentage values are relative to total passenger kilometres in 2018, the base year of the study.
Source: Generated by the authors, using results of simulations from MOLES.

Various policy packages are simulated in the study. These are: the "promote public transport" policy package, which incentivises a switch to bus and rail transport though road pricing mechanisms and fare subsidies; the "promote electric vehicles" policy package, which exempts electric vehicles from heightened operational costs imposed on conventional vehicles; and various densification packages that relax maximum density regulations.

Results indicate that these policy packages provide effective pathways to reduce emissions from urban road transport in Auckland. The public transport package is found to reduce aggregate emissions by 40% in 2050, relative to the reference case, while the electric vehicle package reduces aggregate emissions by 30% in 2050. Reforming land-use regulations can enhance the emission reductions achieved by transport policies. For instance, a general relaxation of density regulations in Auckland can reduce emissions by an additional 10% when implemented in combination with policies that promote public transport and electric vehicles. These results are presented at an aggregate and *per capita* level in Figure 5.2.

Figure 5.2. Emissions from urban transport in the different policy scenarios

Percentage values are relative to emissions in 2018, the base year of the study.

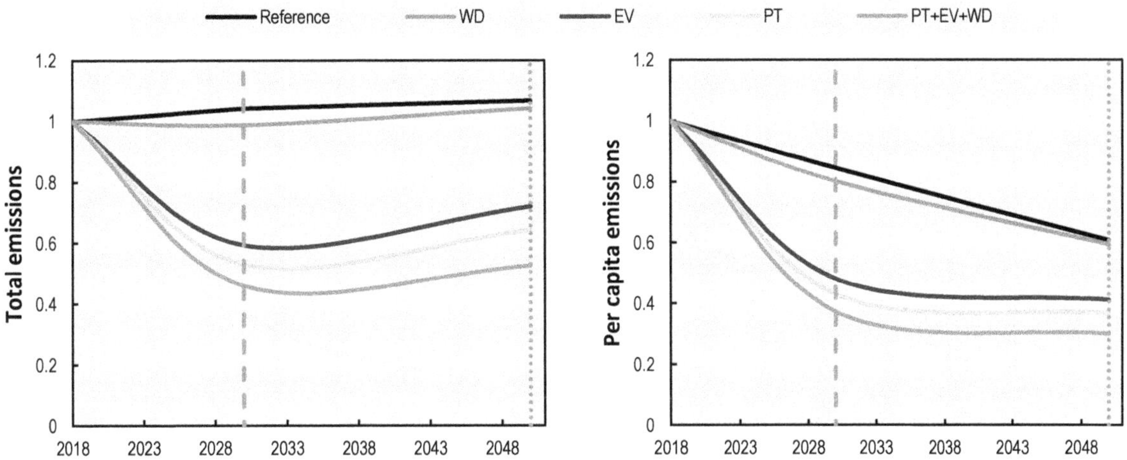

Note: Left panel: total emissions; right panel: per capita emissions. WD refers to a scenario of widespread relaxation of density regulations; EV refers to a scenario where the "promote electric vehicles" policy package is active; PT refers to a scenario where the "promote public transport" policy package is active; PT+EV+WD refers to a scenario where all three policy packages are active. See Chapter 2 for details on the components of the policy packages.
Source: Generated by the authors, using results of simulations from MOLES.

The measures to support the adoption of EVs are composed of instruments that increase the price of owning and operating a conventional vehicle. They also include subsidies, which reduce the private cost of owning and operating an electric vehicle. These policy components have a moderate effect in the ownership rate of EVs. In 2050 in the reference scenario, 78.4% of modelled households own a conventional vehicle, 10.6% do not own a vehicle and 10.9% own an electric vehicle. In particular, the policy package that supports electric vehicles over conventional vehicles increases the EV ownership share to 13.3% from 10.9% it would otherwise be (reference scenario) in 2050. The reason for this moderate response is that the non-modelled advantages of conventional vehicles over EVs are not affected by the policy package. This is explored in more detail in section 5.2 and 5.3.

While the rate of EV ownership responds moderately to the policy package, the share of total passenger kilometres generated by EVs increases substantially. This occurs because the policies described above render EV use much cheaper relative to ICE vehicles. The changes to modal split and passenger kilometres by mode are presented in Figure 5.3.

Figure 5.3. Electric vehicles as a share of ownership and passenger kilometres

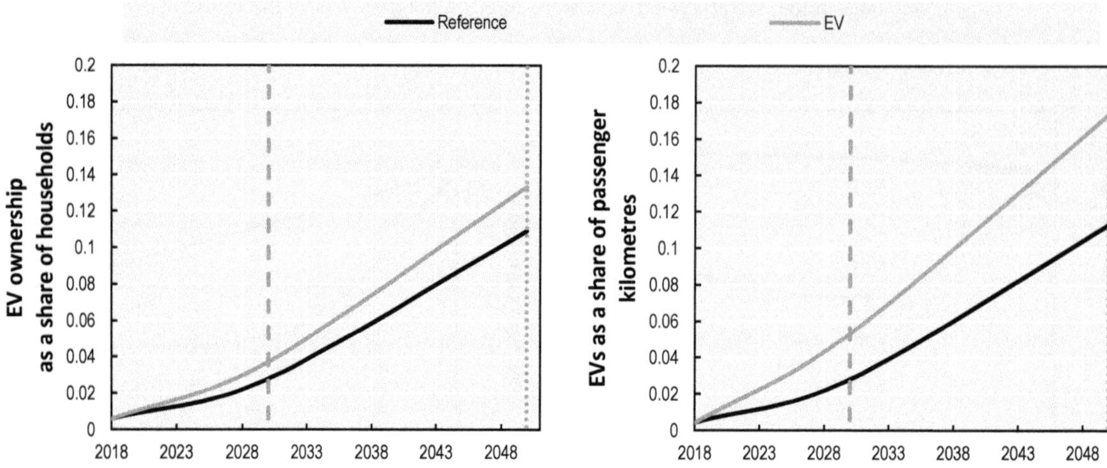

Note: Left panel: electric vehicles as a share of vehicle ownership; right panel: electric vehicles as a share of passenger kilometres.
Source: Generated by the authors, using results of simulations from MOLES.

Similarly, the channels through which the "promote public transport" package reduces emissions relative to the reference case can be evaluated. The package induces a 3.1% increase in the number of households that will choose not to own a vehicle in 2050. The rigidity of the ownership rate of private vehicles can be attributed to a series of non-pecuniary disadvantages of public transport. The low frequency of service and poor connectivity of public transport in low-density areas are two examples of such disadvantages.

The "promote public transport" policy package induces a significant change in the composition of passenger kilometres. In 2050, the share of passenger kilometres undertaken by public transport modes increases to 33.6%, from 7.6% in the reference case. This implies that the majority of households choose to retain the option of owning a private vehicle, possibly in order to use it for certain trips, but alter their commuting behaviour in favour of public transport.

The increase in passenger kilometres caused by the "promote public transport" package is even more pronounced in 2030. This can be explained by the fact that both conventional and electric vehicles become more attractive as fuel economy and energy efficiency increases. In contrast, the attributes of public transport remain fixed throughout the period. This means that public transport is relatively more attractive in 2030 than in 2050 where technological developments has improved the characteristics of conventional and electric vehicles. The share of households which do not own a vehicle and the share of passenger kilometres undertaken by public transport is presented in Figure 5.4.

Figure 5.4. Share of households that do not own a private vehicle and public transport as a share of total passenger kilometres

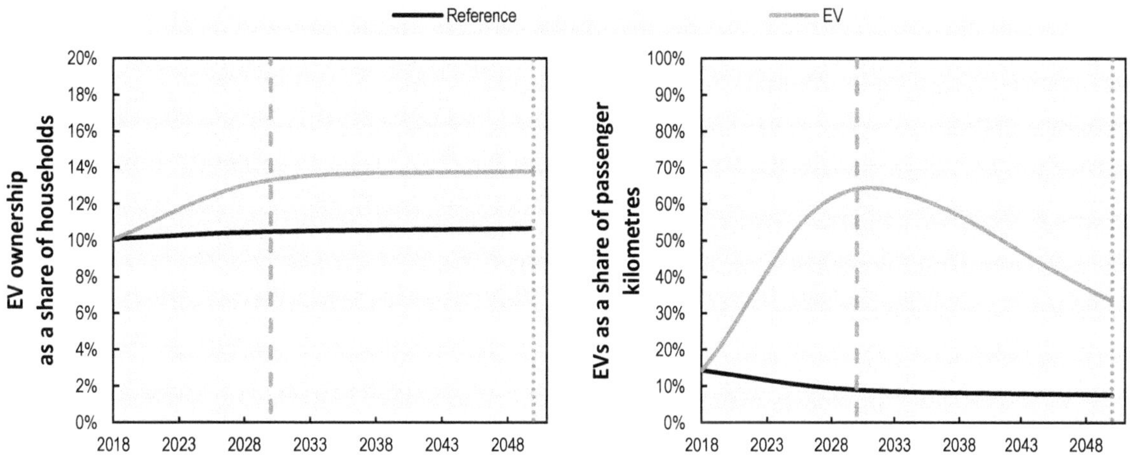

Note: Left panel: no vehicle ownership as a share of households; right panel: public transport as a share of passenger kilometres.
Source: Generated by the authors, using results of simulations from MOLES.

This section has briefly highlighted the main changes in vehicle use and emissions prompted by changes in technology, demographics and policy. Sections 5.2 and 5.3 explain the mechanisms driving these changes in detail and present the environmental, fiscal and distributional implications of the different scenarios.

5.2. Analysis of the reference scenario

5.2.1. Evolution of policies under the reference scenario

The reference scenario models a "business-as-usual" evolution of the key policies that affect emissions from urban transport. These policies include a set of rather moderate taxes on vehicle ownership, as well as on vehicle and fuel use. They also include limited support for EV uptake and the persistence of relatively high public transport fares. Therefore, the switch to less carbon-intensive modes of urban transport is not highly incentivised in the reference scenario.

At the same time, the reference scenario assumes a particularly slow fade-out of the unmeasured advantages of ICE vehicles *vis-à-vis* EVs. The scenario assumes that the technological progress will bridge part of the gap between ICE vehicles and EVs. Among others, that translates into an evolution of the factors that are not directly quantified in the modelling exercise: a growing variety of affordable EVs, a shorter average charging time and cheaper spare parts. However, the reference case assumes that, due to a rather weak policy support for innovation in the EV industry, the pace of that evolution will be moderate. Consequently, the difference in consumer utility derived from the non-quantified features that differ between ICE and EVs will fall by approximately 2% per year over the period 2018-2050. This means that roughly 45% of the non-modelled advantage that ICE vehicles possess *vis-à-vis* EVs is preserved in 2050.

Finally, the reference scenario assumes that the large comparative advantage of ICE vehicles vis-à-vis public transport modes will fall only slightly. This advantage stems from negative non-pecuniary attributes that characterise public transport. They include waiting times, connections, walking distances, as well as the frequency and reliability of service. The reference scenario assumes that these attributes improve at a very slow pace. As a result of the public transport system's gradual improvement, the gap in consumer utility derived from the non-quantified features that differ between public transport and all other modes slowly narrows with time. That is, it reduces at a pace that lies between 2% and 3% per year in the period 2018-2050. The evolution of the utility from the non-quantified attributes of ICE vehicles, EVs and public transport is displayed in Figure 5.5. This assumption is highly significant for the overall results. The effect of adopting a more optimistic view regarding the non-quantified advantage of ICE vehicles vis-à-vis EVs and public transport over time is tested in the sensitivity analysis presented in Chapter 6.

Figure 5.5. Evolution of utility from non-quantified differences between different modes of transport.

The non-quantified utility of an ICE vehicle and an EV evolve over time.

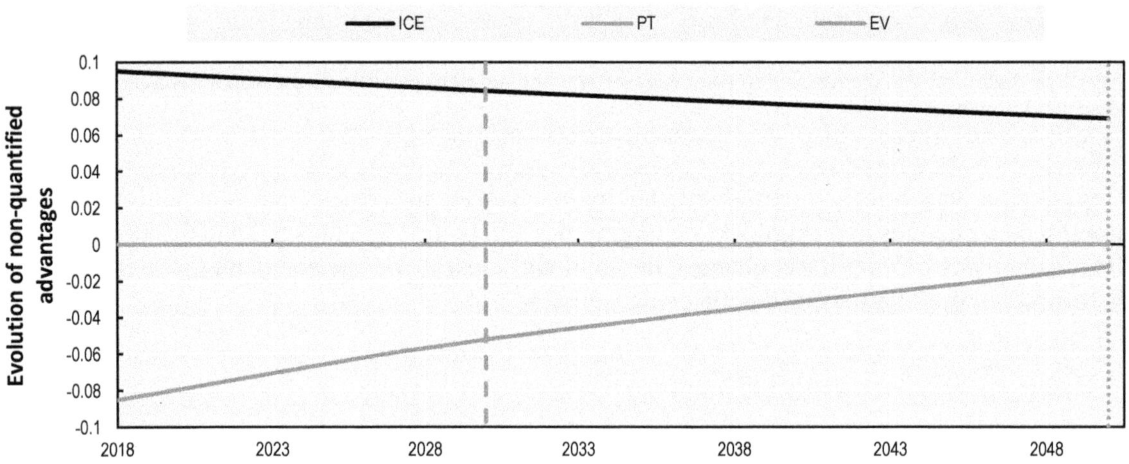

Note: As the modelling exercise is based exclusively on *utility differences*, the unobserved utility of public transport is set to zero and used as reference.
Source: Generated by the authors, using results of simulations from MOLES.

5.2.2. Vehicle use and emissions

The assumptions about EVs in the reference scenario give rise to a path in which private ICE vehicles remain the dominant mode of urban transport. The evolution of the modal split in the reference scenario is shown in Figure 5.6. The share of EVs in the fleet increases from 0.5% in the benchmark year (2018) to 2.8% in 2030 and to 10.9% in 2050. That growth is coupled with a gradual decrease of the share of ICE vehicles in the modal split, which decreases from 89.3% in 2018 to 86.7% in 2030 and to 78.4% in 2050. The share of households that do not own a vehicle remains relatively stable, i.e. it is 10.6% in 2050. The corresponding share of passenger kilometres by ICE vehicles, EVs and public transport is shown in Figure 5.7.

Figure 5.6. Ownership modal split

The share of EVs increases gradually to 11% and the share of ICE vehicles declines to 78%.

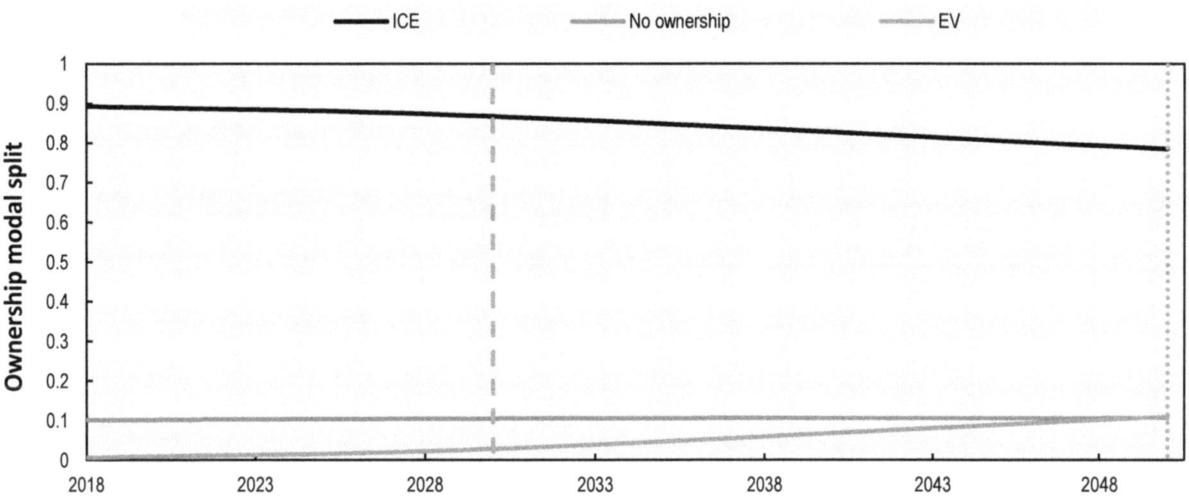

Source: Generated by the authors, using results of simulations from MOLES.

Figure 5.7. Composition of passenger kilometres

The evolution of the share of passenger kilometres made by ICE vehicles, EVs and public transport.

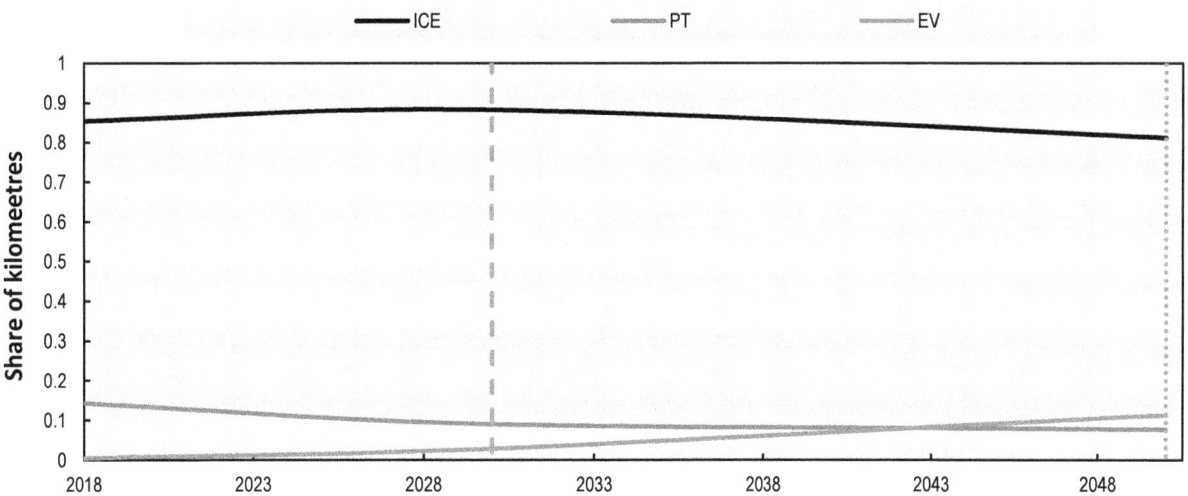

Source: Generated by the authors, using results of simulations from MOLES.

The reference scenario predicts that the total greenhouse gas emissions from urban transport will continue growing. Relative to the 2018 levels, these emissions will have increased by 4% in 2030 and by 7% in 2050. The projected trend of the total emissions from urban transport, relative to their respective value in 2018, is shown by the solid grey curve in Figure 5.8. In the same figure, the rest of the curves represent the greenhouse gas emissions attributed to ICE vehicles, EVs and public transport. These are also expressed relative to the total amount of greenhouse gas emissions in 2018. In 2050, the projection shows that almost all (99.4%) of the emissions from urban transport in Auckland will be generated by the use of ICE vehicles. This is indicated by the convergence of the curves representing ICE and total emissions respectively.

Figure 5.8. Greenhouse gas emissions from urban transport

Evolution of total emissions and their components.

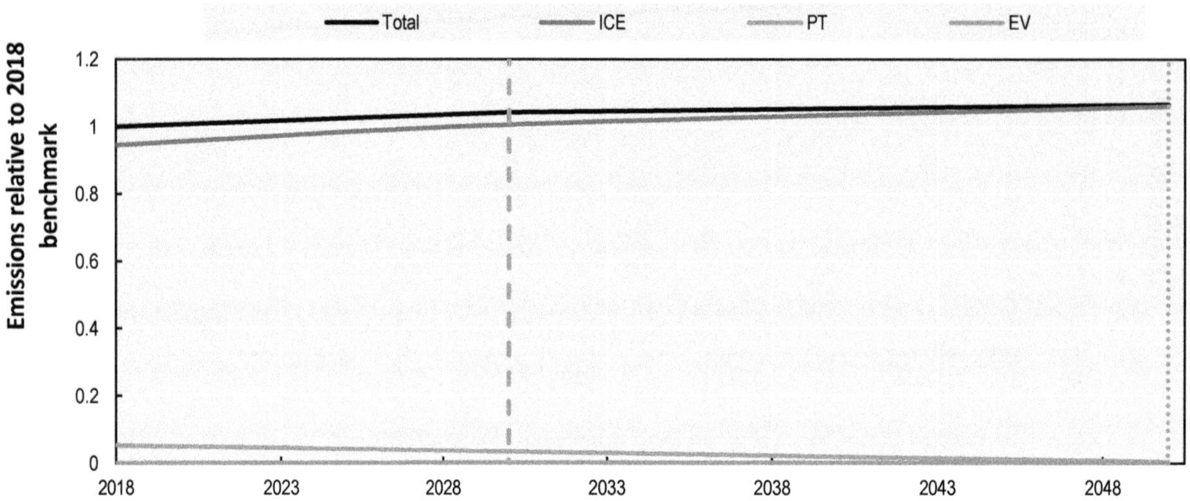

Note: All emissions are reported relative to the total emissions from urban transport in year 2018. The grey curve expresses the total emissions from urban transport as a fraction of the respective emissions in 2018. The three black curves (solid, short dashed and long dashed) decompose the total emissions into those originating from internal combustion engine (ICE), electric (EV) and public transport vehicles.
Source: Generated by the authors, using results of simulations from MOLES.

Three critical assumptions underlie this finding. First, the carbon intensity of the electricity generation in New Zealand will continue decreasing, from 0.12 kg of CO_2e per kWh in 2018 to 0.02 kg of CO_2e per kWh in 2050. Second, the electricity consumption of a representative EV is assumed to fall considerably. From a starting value of 0.17 kWh in 2018 it falls to 0.09 kWh per km in 2050. Thus, the amount of CO_2e generated per kilometre by an EV in 2050 is less than 10% of the respective amount in 2018. Finally, all urban public transport modes in 2050 are assumed to be electrified in line with the planned policies to reduce emissions from public transport (Auckland Transport, 2018[2]). Therefore, policies that target greenhouse gas emissions should focus on reducing the kilometres of any existing ICE fleet and on accelerating its replacement by EVs.

The growth in greenhouse gas emissions displayed in Figure 5.8 is partially driven by a substantial increase in population. That increase is approximately 75% in the period 2018-2050. To understand how total greenhouse gas emissions from urban transport could evolve in a city characterised by no population growth, Figure 5.9 displays the *per capita* CO_2e emissions in Auckland. These emissions, which are expressed relative to their value in 2018, are projected to fall by roughly 40% in 2050. The largest part of this decline is due to improvements in the fuel efficiency of ICE vehicles, which is projected to increase by 55% between 2018 and 2050. The analysis presented in Figure 5.8 and Figure 5.9 indicates that the technological evolution in the industries of ICE vehicles and EVs will most likely fall short of delivering carbon neutrality in transport sector by 2050.

Figure 5.9. ***Per capita*** **greenhouse gas emissions from urban transport**

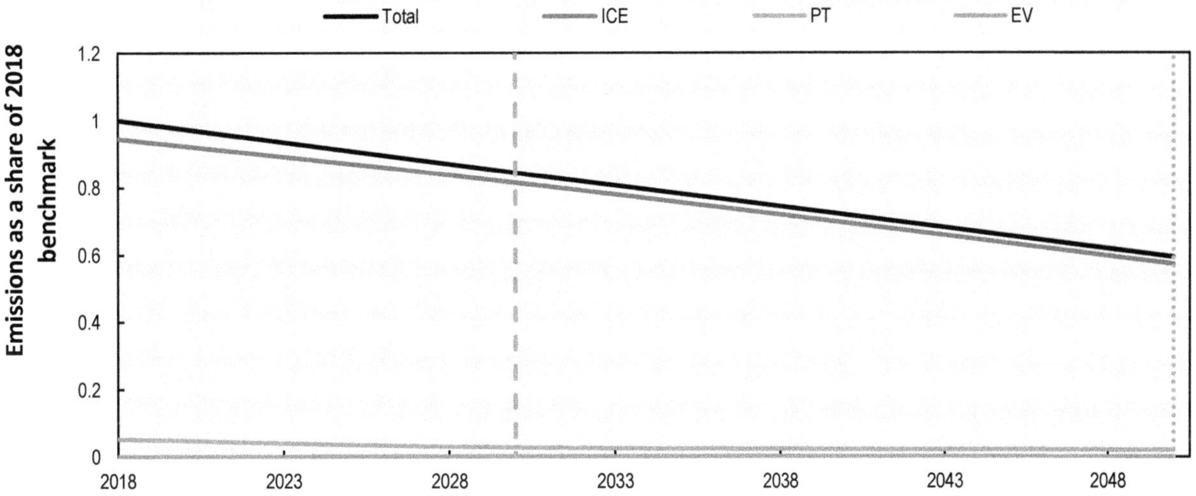

Note: *Per capita* emissions are reported relative to the *per capita* emissions from urban transport in year 2018. The grey curve expresses *per capita* emissions from urban transport as a fraction of the respective emissions in 2018. The three black curves (solid, short dashed and long dashed) decompose these relative total emissions into those originating from internal combustion engine (ICE), electric (EV) and public transport vehicles.
Source: Generated by the authors, using results of simulations from MOLES.

5.2.3. The evolution of urban form, housing prices and affordability

The evolution of transport-related greenhouse gas emissions is closely linked to two factors: the evolution of urban form and the level of housing supply. In the reference scenario, urban form evolves through the gradual increase in population density in existing areas. It also changes through the conversion of designated future urban areas to residential areas. The development pattern in newly developed areas is similar to that of existing residential areas. The development pattern in existing residential areas remains intact.

The gradual increase in population density is presented in Figure 5.10. Population density in 2050 is higher than in 2018. This is illustrated by the increased prevalence of darker colours, which indicate areas of higher population density. The right panel of Figure 5.10 includes several new residential areas. Employment evolves in a similar manner. Figure 5.11 displays the evolution of job density by employment zone. In 2050, the employment areas remain the same as in 2018 but employ more people.

Figure 5.10. Evolution of population density by residential zone

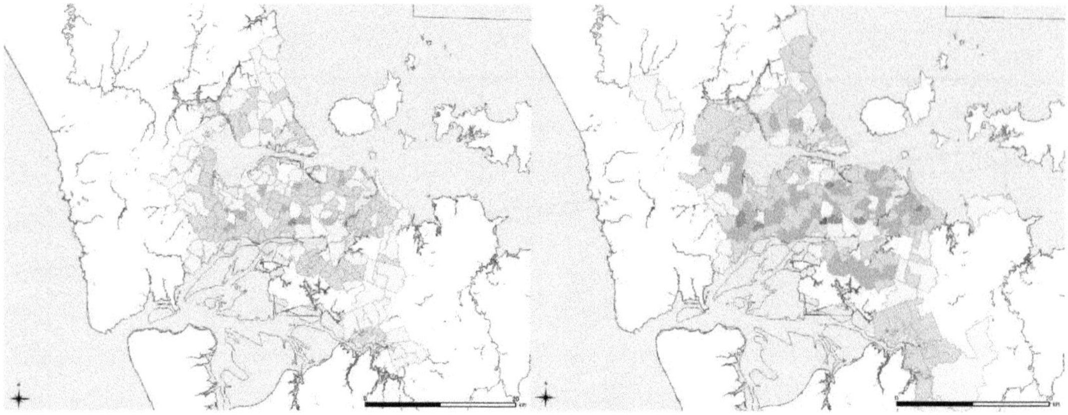

Note: Left panel: population density in 2018; right panel: population density in 2050. Darker colours represent area units with higher population density.
Source: Generated by the authors, using results of simulations from MOLES.

Figure 5.11. Evolution of job density by employment zone

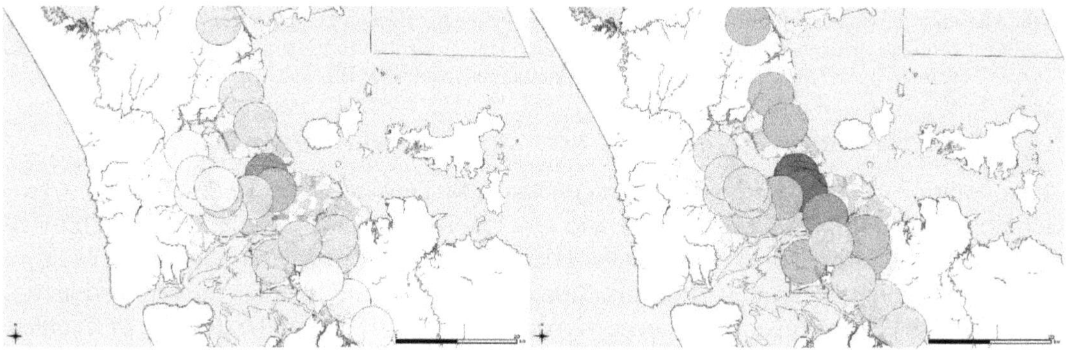

Note: Left panel: employment density in 2018; right panel: employment density in 2050. Darker colours represent areas of higher employment density.
Source: Generated by the authors, using results of simulations from MOLES.

Housing supply evolves according to the patterns established in the existing urban form and is a key determinant of housing prices and housing affordability. The impact of policies targeting housing supply may be twofold, as they are likely to affect housing prices and the environmental performance of a city.

The reference scenario predicts that the average housing prices in Auckland will steadily increase between 2018 and 2050. Compared to 2018, real housing prices will have increased by at least 50% by 2030 and by more than 200% by 2050. This steep increase is displayed in Figure 5.12. The projection implies an average growth rate of real prices that is approximately 3.6% per year. The findings from the simulation of the reference scenario are in line with the observations from the 32-year period that preceded the benchmark year, i.e. the period 1985-2017 (The Economist, 2019[3]). During that period, real average housing prices in Auckland increased between 200% and 300%. Furthermore, in the 25-year period between 1989 and 2014, the city's population increased by 55%. The annual average growth rate of the population during that period was 1.76%, which is the growth rate assumed in the reference scenario. Finally, the various indicators of urban footprint extent increased between 25% and 32% over the 1989-2014 period, a change that is comparable to the one assumed in the reference scenario.

Figure 5.12. Average real housing prices in Auckland in the reference scenario

Observed and projected evolution of housing prices.

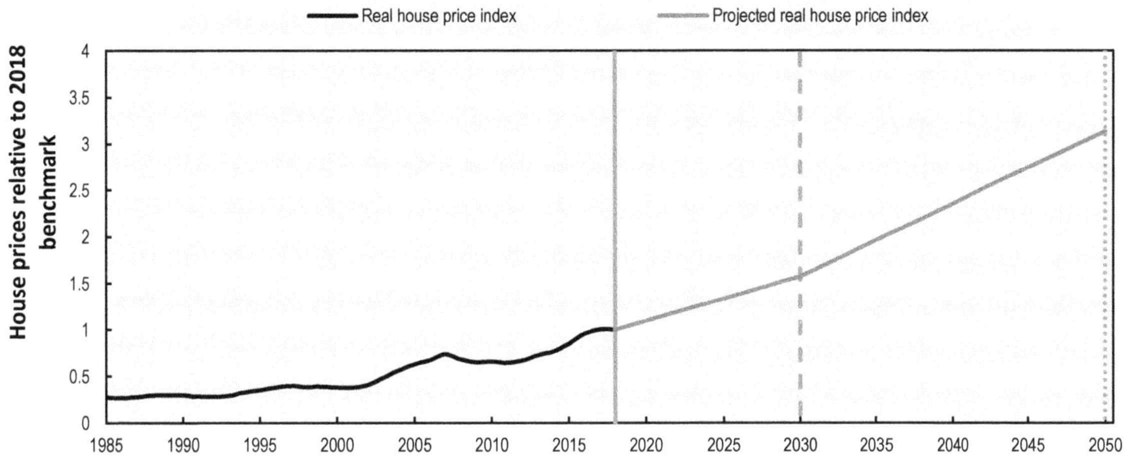

Note: The evolution of the housing price index is computed using the OECD's real house price index. The values displayed in the dotted curve (1985-2017) are expressed relative to New Zealand's housing price index reported in 2017. The projected mean values displayed in the solid curve are expressed relative to the mean housing price in the model's benchmark year (2018). The vertical lines mark the years at which housing prices are computed with MOLES.
Source: Real house price index between 1985 and 2017 uses past time series (The Economist, 2019[3]); the projected real house price index is generated by the authors, using results of simulations from MOLES.

To a large extent, the house price growth in the reference scenario stems from the projected growth in population and in real income. Increases in both variables are known to raise demand for housing and to exert a positive pressure on housing prices. Population and income are projected to be 75% and 54% higher, respectively, in 2050, as shown in Chapter 2.

Most importantly, the reference scenario assumes that urban development continues to take place in a business-as-usual manner. This means that low residential density remains the predominant development pattern in the existing urban fabric, within which housing supply remains constant. Furthermore, in the reference scenario low residential density constitutes the recipe for future development. To keep the simulation results tractable, the reference scenario rules out infill development.

If the steep increase in projected house prices materializes, it will have a significant impact on private budgets. It is also likely to reduce the overall welfare gains expected in the examined period. An alternative interpretation of the simulation results is that the projected increase in housing prices will materialise only partially. This is likely because any substantial house price increase may hamper the expected population growth, which is also a driver of rising house prices. Even in this case, however, part of the expected welfare gains will be foregone, as these gains are linked to the attraction of a highly skilled labour force from other parts of New Zealand and the world. Therefore, growing housing prices and limited housing supply are two interrelated challenges that must be addressed simultaneously.

Given the strong projected growth in housing costs, the simulation of the reference scenario predicts a steep increase in the share of income spent on housing costs. Such a substantial increase will be accompanied by significant distributional impacts, which are likely to be detrimental for some parts of the population. That holds true especially for those with limited borrowing capacity. On the other hand, current landlords with negative net housing expenditure will benefit from the limited growth in housing supply and the associated increase in housing prices.

5.2.4. Fiscal implications

The reference scenario yields important insights on the performance of the set of fiscal instruments considered in the study. The revenues from public transport fares, vehicle licencing fees, kilometre taxes, the excise and *ad-valorem* taxes on gasoline and electricity evolve over time. Some of these revenue changes are more distinct, since the bases of the corresponding taxes undergo more profound changes as the ownership and the kilometre share of each transport mode evolves. Figure 5.13 displays the evolution of the *total* tax revenue and its components, expressing them relative to the total tax revenue in 2018.

Figure 5.13. Total tax and fare revenue

The evolution of revenue from national and local tax instruments and public transport fares.

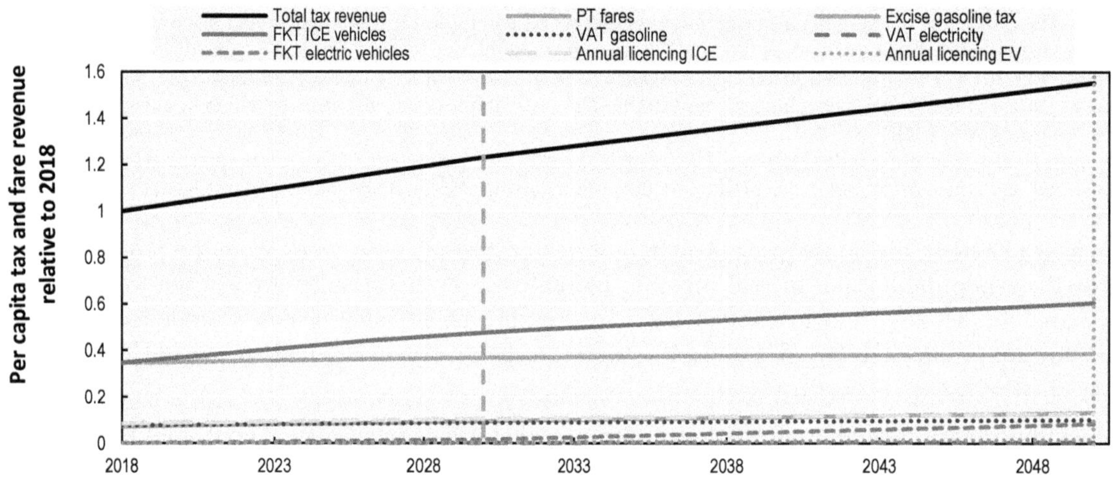

Source: Generated by the authors, using results of simulations from MOLES.

The total revenue from the considered instruments, displayed in the solid black curve of Figure 5.13, increases by approximately 55%. The most important contributor to that is population growth, which is 75% and implies a considerable increase in some tax bases. The corresponding changes of *per capita* revenues are shown in Figure 5.14. Total tax revenue *per capita*, indicated by the thick solid curve in the upper panel of the figure, decreases by 12% in the considered period (2018-2050). One of the most notable findings is that the revenue from the excise tax on gasoline falls. This occurs primarily because the fuel consumption of the remaining ICE vehicles drops substantially, i.e. by 36% in 2050, due to improvements in the fuel efficiency of ICE vehicles. The changes in the revenue from the kilometre tax in ICE vehicles are negligible. A moderate shrinkage of the ICE vehicle fleet (88% of all vehicles in 2050) and a slight increase in travel demand, which offsets the former effect, underlie this finding.

The rest of the tax instruments are shown in the lower panel of Figure 5.14. These make up a substantial part of the total revenue. However, the separate contribution of each of these instruments is small compared to that of the excise gasoline tax and of the ICE vehicle kilometre tax.

The revenues from the annual licencing and circulation fees of ICE vehicles, as well as from the VAT on gasoline, decline. The downward trend of the former can be attributed to the shrinkage of the ICE vehicle fleet. The latter revenue declines as the fuel economy improves, inducing a decrease in fuel consumption.

The revenue from the kilometre tax imposed on EVs increases, as the share of these vehicles in the fleet grows. In 2050, 5-6% of the total tax revenue from the instruments examined in the report will be generated by the kilometre tax on EVs. The revenues from the licencing fees on EVs and from the VAT imposed on their consumed electricity will together account for less than 2% of total tax revenue. This is mainly due to the low levels of annual EV licencing fees. It could also be due to the increasing energy efficiency of EVs. The latter increase offsets part of the increase in electricity consumption that stems from the growth of the EV fleet. Finally, the moderate growth of the share of public transport in the modal split results in a slight increase in the revenue from public transport fares (5.6%).

Figure 5.14. Tax and fare revenue *per capita*

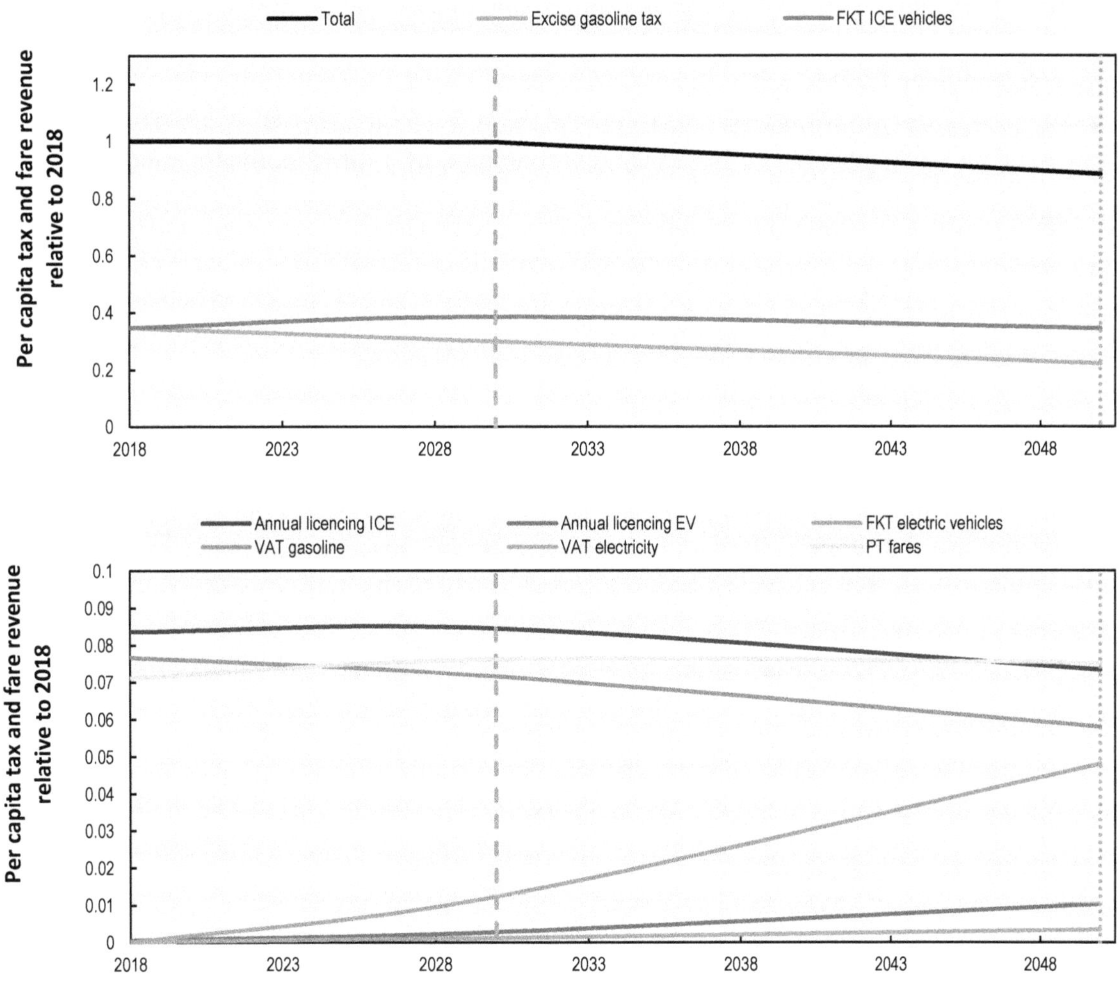

Source: Generated by the authors, using results of simulations from MOLES.

5.3. Analysis of counterfactual scenarios

This section examines the environmental and economic impact of the policy packages described in detail in Chapter 2. Subsection 5.3.1 provides a brief summary of these packages. Subsection 5.3.2 provides an analysis of the environmental and economic impact of counterfactual scenarios based on the implementation of different policy packages.

5.3.1. A brief summary of policy packages

The packages examined in the study are:

- a "***promote public transport***" package. This package contains measures that drastically increase the fixed private costs of both ICE vehicles and EVs. This is done by increasing the annual circulation fees and the operational costs of these vehicles. This is done through a steep increase in the existing kilometre tax and the current level of the excise tax on gasoline. Furthermore, an urban road pricing scheme is introduced in Auckland. The scheme takes the form of a double cordon, with the inner cordon surrounding the central business district and the outer cordon surrounding the inner part of the urban area. The scheme is therefore similar in design to the one introduced in Stockholm. The additional revenue from the aforementioned adjustments suffices not only to provide a drastic subsidy of public transport fares, but also to finance other initiatives. These initiatives are not modelled explicitly, but the analysis derives an approximate measure of the social value of this revenue.
- a "***promote electric vehicles***" package. This package contains a generous subsidy for EVs. That subsidy is a monetary representation of a direct purchase subsidy, e.g. a VAT and annual circulation fee exemption, and of other indirect benefits that EVs may enjoy. These may include the right to use bus lanes, free parking and other benefits, whose effect is not modelled explicitly with MOLES. Moreover, the package introduces a steep increase in the kilometre tax paid by ICE vehicles, but exempts EVs from it. Therefore, it generates a substantial difference in the ownership and operational costs of the two types of vehicles.
- a "***widespread densification***" package. This contains measures that relax the existing density regulations in the city. The package allows buildings to be taller and to occupy a larger share of their land plots. Changes in density are proportional to the existing building height and the land plot coverage (50%) and are uniform across space. Therefore, the supply of residential floor space increases everywhere in the city. However, that increase is more profound in the inner core of the urban area, where structural density is currently higher.
- various "***targeted densification***" packages. These packages substantially relax density regulations in selected areas of the city, while they preserve existing regulations in the rest of the urban fabric. The various packages select the areas to be densified according to different criteria. For example, such criteria may include the proximity to the central business district or the distance from major public transport nodes and employment hubs. The areas selected by each targeted densification package are shown in Figure 5.15.

Figure 5.15. Targeted densification

Four versions of selected densification in Auckland

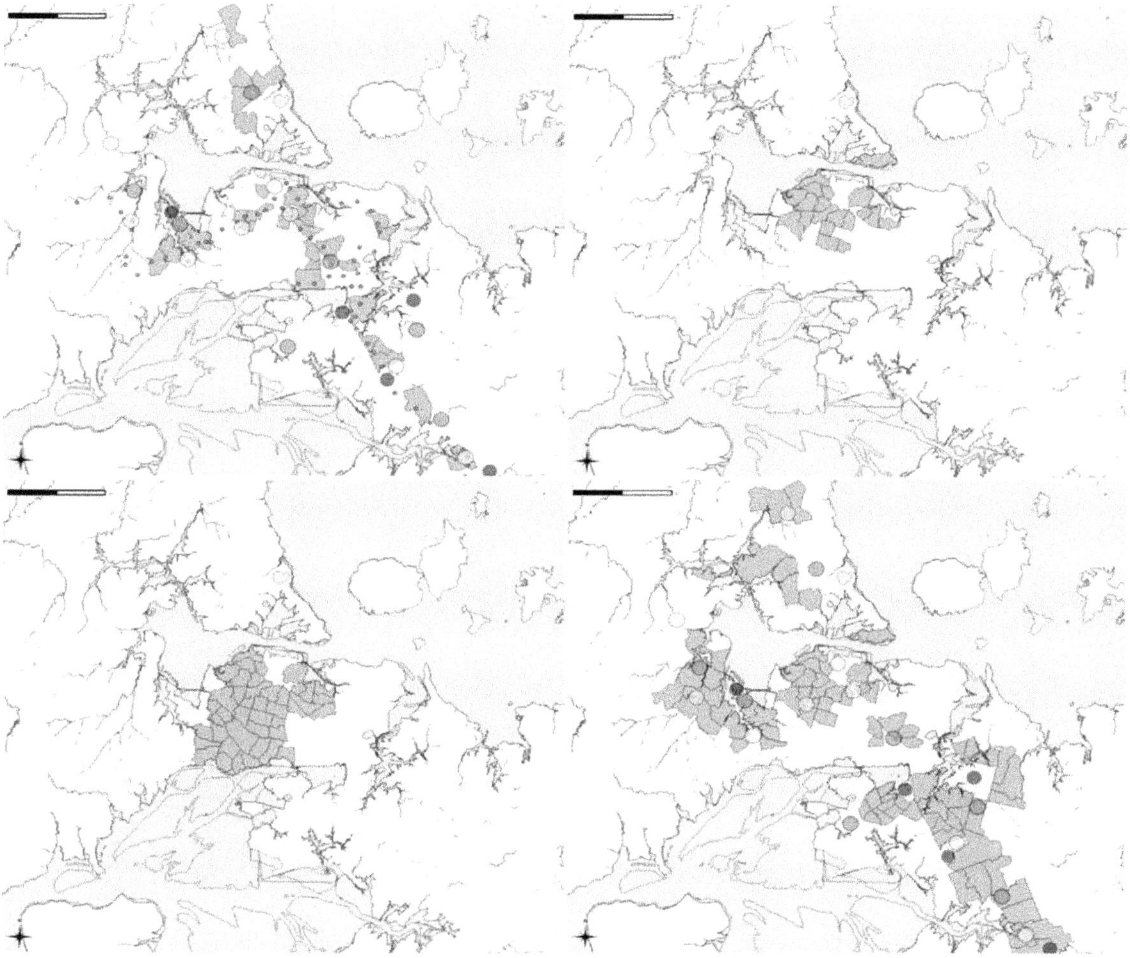

Note: Upper left panel: further densification of already-dense areas lying close to major employment hubs and public transit nodes (TD1); Upper right panel: densification of low-density zones surrounding the central business district (TD2); Lower left panel: densification of low-density areas in Auckland's isthmus (TD3); Lower right panel: densification of areas in close proximity to employment hubs (TD4).
Source: Generated by the authors.

5.3.2. The mid-term (2018-2030) environmental impact of packages

The results presented in this subsection compare the environmental performance of a number of policy packages and their combinations. Each package is evaluated based on its potential to reduce the greenhouse gas emissions from urban transport (CO_2e).

The percentage reductions in CO_2e emissions from the implementation of three policy counterfactual scenarios are displayed in Figure 5.16. These are the "promote public transport" package, the "promote electric vehicles" package and their combination. The reported reductions are expressed relative to the aggregate CO_2e emissions predicted by MOLES for 2030 in the reference scenario. In turn, the reference emissions in 2030 are approximately 4% higher than their value in the benchmark year (2018).

Figure 5.16. Effect of promoting public transport and EVs on emissions in 2030

Estimated percentage of emissions eliminated by promoting public transport, EVs, or both. Percentage values are relative to emissions in the reference case in 2030.

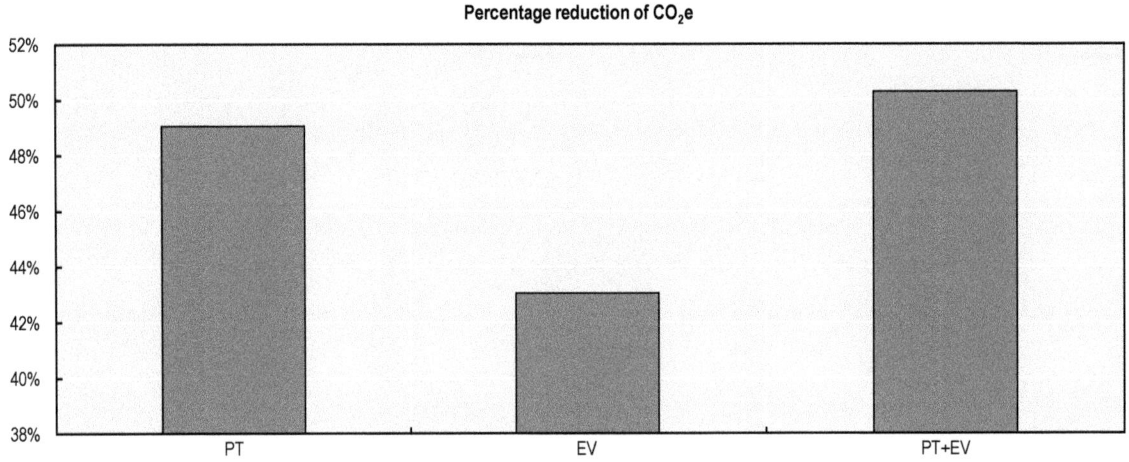

Note: PT refers to the "promote public transport" policy package; EV refers to the "promote electric vehicle" policy package; combinations of the packages are denoted with '+'.
Source: Generated by the authors, using results of simulations from MOLES.

The simulations with MOLES show that both packages, as they are elaborated in Chapter 2, will induce considerable CO_2e reductions. Emissions in 2030 will be 49% lower than their reference level in 2030 with the implementation of the "promote public transport" package. That includes a considerably larger kilometre charge, a steep increase in the ownership and excise gasoline taxes, the introduction of urban road pricing and a generous subsidy of public transport fares. The combination of these drastic interventions induces a 2.5% decrease in the number of households that will choose to own a vehicle in 2030. That rigid response can be attributed to the large relative disadvantages of existing public transport services in low-density areas. Among others, these disadvantages include the low frequency of service and poor connectivity. These are not taken into explicit account in the simulations, but they may explain a large part of the modal split in ownership. Without policies to substantially reduce these disadvantages, the ownership modal split will remain relatively unresponsive to policies that promote public transport only *via* reductions in pecuniary costs, i.e. without improving the quality of the service. In spite of that, the policy components included in the "promote public transport" package can induce a significant change in the composition of passenger kilometres. In 2030, the share of passenger kilometres undertaken by public transport modes can be increased from the reference level of 9.3% to 64.1%. The third column of Table 5.1 displays these changes.

Furthermore, Figure 5.16 suggests that 43% of the reference greenhouse gas emissions in 2030 can be eliminated with the implementation of the "promote electric vehicles" package. That package incorporates the same measures as the "promote public transport" package, but contains three policy components that substantially alter the relative costs between EVs, ICE vehicles and public transport. First, EVs are exempt from all road charges and urban tolls. Second, they are provided a considerable annual subsidy, which is a monetary representation of several non-pecuniary benefits these vehicles may receive (e.g. preferential parking or use of bus lanes). Finally, public transport subsidies are not considered in this package.

Table 5.1. Key modal split changes induced by emission-reducing policies

	Reference	PT	EV	PT + EV
% not owning a private vehicle	10.8%	13.3%	10.7%	13.0%
% km generated with public transport	9.3%	64.1%	46.8%	59.9%
% owning an EV	2.8%	2.6%	3.7%	4.5%
% km generated with an EV	2.8%	1.3%	5.3%	6.6%

Note: PT refers to the "promote public transport" policy package; EV refers to the "promote electric vehicle" policy package.
Source: Generated by the authors.

The policy measures described above increase the attractiveness of EVs, but have a modest effect on their ownership rate, as Table 5.1 suggests. That is, the rate of EV ownership increases from 2.8% it is in 2030 in the reference scenario to 3.7%. The reason for this moderate response is that the non-modelled disadvantages of EVs (e.g. limited range and availability of charging stations) that are part of the vehicle choice decision remain considerable in 2030 (Figure 5.5). In spite of this, the "promote electric vehicles" policy package is capable of inducing substantial changes in the share of kilometres generated by EVs. This occurs because once an EV has been purchased, the package renders its use much cheaper than it would otherwise be. Furthermore, the package contains all the components that discourage the use of ICE vehicles. As such, the "promote electric vehicles" package drastically increases the share of passenger kilometres generated by public transport. That increase, i.e. from 9.3% to 46.8%, is comparable but somewhat smaller than the one induced by the "promote public transport" policy package (64.1%).

The last column of Table 5.1 displays the effects from the simultaneous implementation of the two aforementioned packages. In that case, generous subsidies are provided both to public transport and to EV use. The findings suggest that some of the measures contained in these two packages may have an antagonistic effect with respect to the outcomes of interest. For example, efforts to promote EVs can reduce the passenger kilometres travelled *via* public transport modes, if they render EVs more attractive than public transport. For this reason, any potential synergies between these two policy packages are likely to be limited in size.

Combining the "promote public transport" package, as elaborated above, with a densification package may yield larger cuts in greenhouse gas emissions from urban transport. Figure 5.17 highlights the additional impact of targeted and widespread densification. The largest additional emission reductions (6.3%) are generated by a targeted densification program that increases residential density around the largest employment hubs. That package has significant emissions reduction potential as a stand-alone measure (-14%), but this potential is even greater when it is combined with policies that actively encourage the greater use of public transport.

A similarly considerable effect is generated by widespread densification, which relaxes density regulations everywhere within the urban area. However, as explained in detail in Chapter 2, the uniform relaxation of density coefficients generates more additional floor space in areas where density is relatively higher. These constitute mainly central areas that lie relatively closer to key points of activity, such as jobs and large shopping hubs.

For reasons that are expanded upon in the next section, only the targeted densification programs TD2 and TD3 are welfare improving. These densify the areas surrounding the central business district and the low-density parts of Auckland's inner core, respectively. Additional emission reductions in 2030 relative to the reference scenario will be 1.7% and 3.7%, respectively.

Figure 5.17. The mid-term (2018-2030) environmental impact of the "promote public transport" policy package and the various densification programmes

The CO_2e reductions from promoting public transport as a stand-alone policy or in combination with a densification program. Percentage values are relative to emissions in the reference case in 2030.

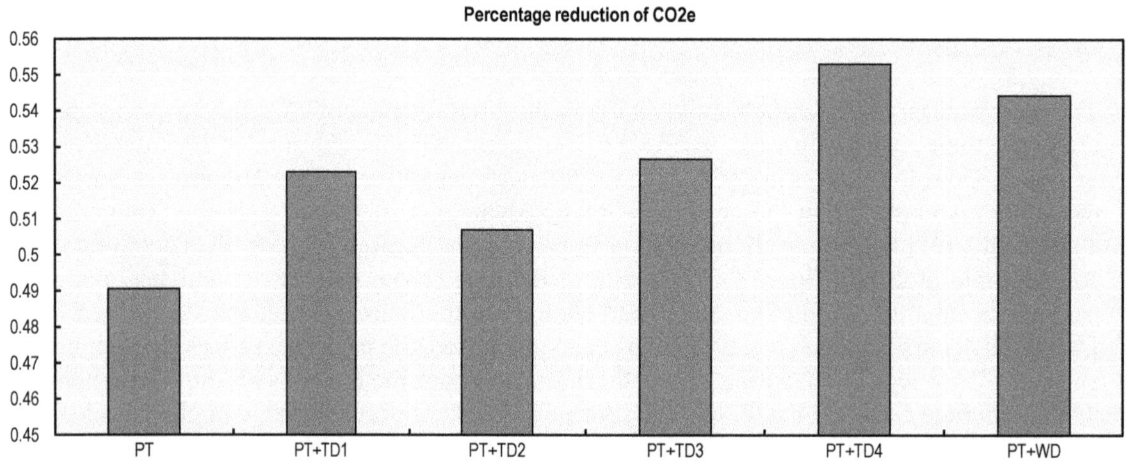

Note: PT refers to the "*promote public transport*" policy package; EV refers to the "*promote electric vehicle*" policy package; WD refers to a *widespread densification* program; TD refers to a *targeted densification* program; combinations of the packages are denoted with '+'.
Source: Generated by the authors, using results of simulations from MOLES.

5.3.3. The mid-term (2018-2030) welfare impact of packages

The analysis in the previous subsection focused on the environmental impacts of the policy packages examined in the study. This subsection highlights the potential trade-offs between environmental and economic performance and identifies the policies that achieve both objectives.

The values displayed in Figure 5.18 are monetised welfare gains associated with a selection of policy packages and their combinations. The welfare calculations, described in full detail in Chapter 3, are based on three measures. The first is the compensating variation of each policy. That measure is the amount of money households need to be compensated with, *ex-post* to the implementation of the policy, in order to be equally well-off as in the reference case. The second component of welfare is the social cost (respectively, benefit) from the fiscal deficit (respectively, surplus) that the package generates *vis-à-vis* the reference case. The final component is the social cost (respectively, benefit) from the carbon emission increases (respectively, reductions) the package generates *vis-à-vis* the reference case. The sum of these measures yields the welfare gain (or loss) of a policy, which is expressed relative to the projected average income in the considered year.

Figure 5.18. The mid-term (2018-2030) economic impact of recommended policies

The annual welfare gains *per capita* (net of environmental benefits) from promoting public transport, EVs and selected densification of low-density areas around the central business district.

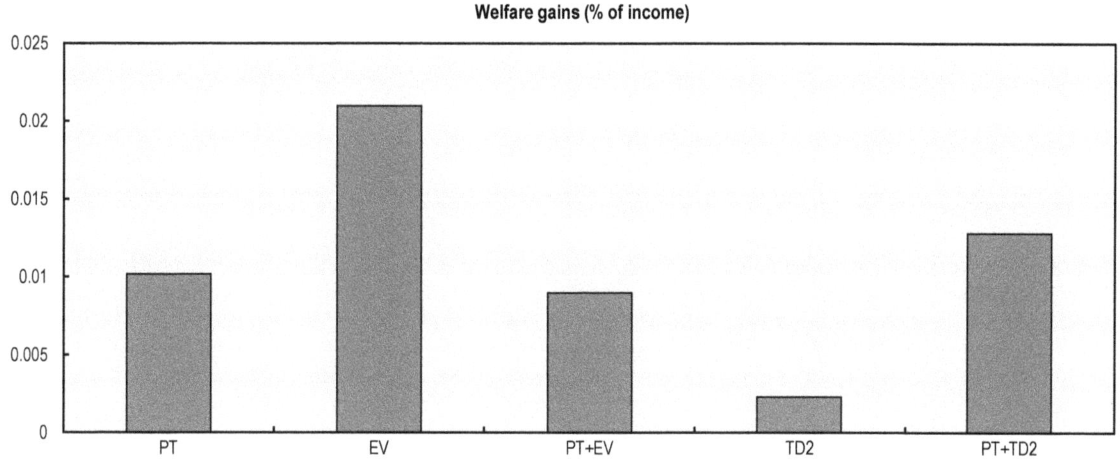

Note: PT refers to the "promote public transport" policy package; EV refers to the "promote electric vehicle" policy package; WD refers to a widespread densification program; TD refers to a targeted densification program; different combinations of the packages are denoted with '+'.
Source: Generated by the authors, using results of simulations from MOLES.

In 2030, both "promote electric vehicles" and the "promote public transport" packages are effective, not only in reducing emissions but also in generating a substantial welfare benefit. Promoting EVs increases social welfare by 2.1% of income. A large part of the welfare gain originates from the reduction of traffic and congestion. The package generates these gains because the ownership and use of private ICE vehicles are heavily taxed. A similar effect is generated by the "promote public transport" package. However, that package offers a significant subsidy to public transport modes without generating substantial additional benefits in terms of congestion relief. Furthermore, these large subsidies give rise to a much lower net revenue.[1]

Densification of low-density areas around the city's central business district is welfare increasing as a stand-alone package. The package constitutes a mild densification program that increases housing supply in the areas surround the Central Business District as shown in the upper right panel of Figure 5.15. These areas lie close to jobs, shopping malls and other key trip destinations. The program leaves the development pattern in the rest of the suburban areas intact. In this way, it accommodates the high demand for private open space, which is generated by the part of the population with a strong preference for low-density development. Combining this mild densification program (TD2) with the measures that promote public transport yields an annual gain equivalent to 1.3% of income.

Figure 5.19. The mid-term (2018-2030) economic impact of promoting public transport and densification

The annual welfare gains or losses *per capita* (net of environmental benefits) from promoting public transport as a stand-alone policy or in combination with a densification program.

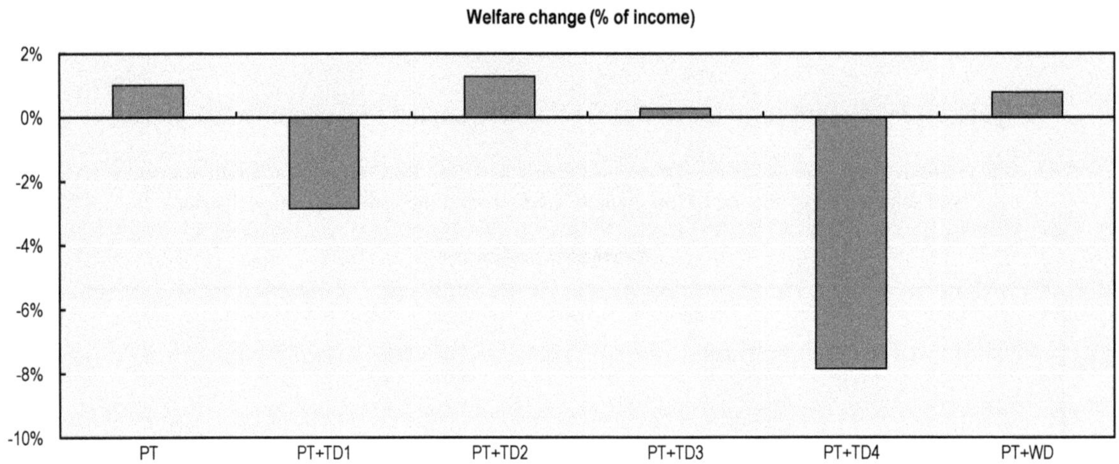

Note: PT refers to the *"promote public transport"* policy package; EV refers to the *"promote electric vehicle"* policy package; WD refers to a widespread densification program; TD refers to a targeted densification program; TD1 refers to further densification of already-dense areas lying close to major employment hubs and public transit nodes; TD2 refers to densification of low-density zones surrounding the central business district; TD3 refers to densification of low-density areas in Auckland's isthmus; TD4 refers to densification of areas in close proximity to employment hubs; different combinations of the packages are denoted with '+'.
Source: Generated by the authors, using results of simulations from MOLES.

5.3.4. Policy recommendations for the mid-term (2018-2030)

The following general recommendations, which refer to the period from 2018 to 2030, can be extracted from the findings:

- **Implement immediate measures to reduce the use of private vehicles and congestion.** The findings of the study show that minor increases of the kilometre charge and the environmental component (ETS) of the gasoline tax are not sufficient to reduce greenhouse gas emissions from urban transport considerably. The model simulations suggest that sizeable increases in the kilometre charge (e.g. NZD 0.50) and the excise gasoline tax (e.g. NZD 1.00) are needed to induce a significant shift to public transport.

- **Finance electric vehicle benefits through an increase of the annual costs of ICE vehicle ownership.** Annual circulation fees are relatively low in New Zealand. Their gradual increase could finance investments in support infrastructure for EVs, such as recharging stations.

- **Improve the quality of public transport system services.** To facilitate the transition from private vehicle use to public transport ridership, the local public transport system has to be upgraded. It should become less fragmented and more reliable, in order to provide a viable alternative to private vehicle use. Increasing the frequency of service in areas where population density is relatively high would be particularly effective. Comfort is another important non-pecuniary attribute that should also be taken into consideration by policy makers.

- **Introduce a mild densification program that intensifies gradually.** Reforms of land-use regulations could take the form of removing building height restrictions and other regulations in low-density areas around the CBD. This mild densification program should intensify gradually, as population increases and the demand for residential floor space causes housing prices to rise even further. Once this occurs, low-density areas other than those surrounding the CBD can be incorporated in the densification program. For example, these areas could include the low-density areas within the isthmus. Alternatively, such a program may take the form of a marginal relaxation of density regulations in the entire urban fabric.
- **Delay the development of disconnected areas.** Focus development in urban areas rather than periurban areas. Accommodate a larger part of the current housing demand with infill development.
- **Prepare the ground for widespread densification programs to be introduced in the long run**. Accommodating both a large increase in population and the strong preference for low-density development is likely to be incompatible with the goals of housing affordability and transport decarbonisation. A widespread densification program, which is going to be necessary to curb house price growth in the long run, should be introduced gradually. Local and national authorities need to prepare the ground for this transition by aligning their policies and harmonising their objectives. This process may be subject to multiple rigidities and sources of inertia, thus preparation for densification programs should be made early on.

5.3.5. The long-run (2030-2050) environmental performance of policy packages

This subsection presents the findings from policy simulations run for the second period considered in the study. This period is referred to as the long run and spans the years between 2030 and 2050.

The environmental impacts of packages for the promotion of public transport, electric vehicles and the combination of both are displayed in Figure 5.20. All packages provide considerable reductions from the reference level of emissions in 2050. The magnitude of these reductions are comparable to those obtained in the mid-term.

However, the capacity of the same measures to reduce emissions in the mid- and the long run differs widely. For instance, the "promote public transport" package, which is found to reduce greenhouse gas emissions by 49% in the mid-term, is found to be somewhat less efficient in the long run. The same holds for the policies designed to promote electric vehicles (43% versus 32%).

Fuel efficiency is the main driver behind the reduced environmental effectiveness of packages in the long run. As conventional vehicles become more fuel-efficient, they consume less gasoline for a given distance, which in turn offsets part of the tax burden imposed by the two packages.

A widespread densification program, which is shown to induce large improvements in welfare, can play an important role in restoring the long-run effectiveness of the examined packages. For example, Figure 5.20 shows that combining widespread densification with the promotion of public transport reduces greenhouse gas emissions by 48.4%. That value lies very close to the one reported for the "promote public transport" policy package in the mid-term (49%). Therefore, promoting a compact urban form may be part of the answer to the declining environmental performance of transport policies in the long run.

A widespread densification program, as described in Chapter 2, does not increase density proportionally across urban space. In contrast, more residential floor space is generated in central, than in peripheral areas. This is because the program adjusts the density coefficients in a way that produces more additional residential space in land plots containing attached single family or multifamily buildings. Typically, the areas where these types of (denser) development are more prevalent are also the areas that are served relatively more frequent by public transport. Very often, these areas also lie closer to large employment hubs. Therefore, by densifying these zones further, widespread densification reduces car dependency and the vehicle kilometres travelled.

Figure 5.20. Emission reductions from promoting public transport, EVs and widespread densification in the long run (2030-2050)

Estimated percentage of emissions eliminated by promoting public transport, EVs, or both (2030-2050). Percentage values are relative to emissions in the reference case in 2050.

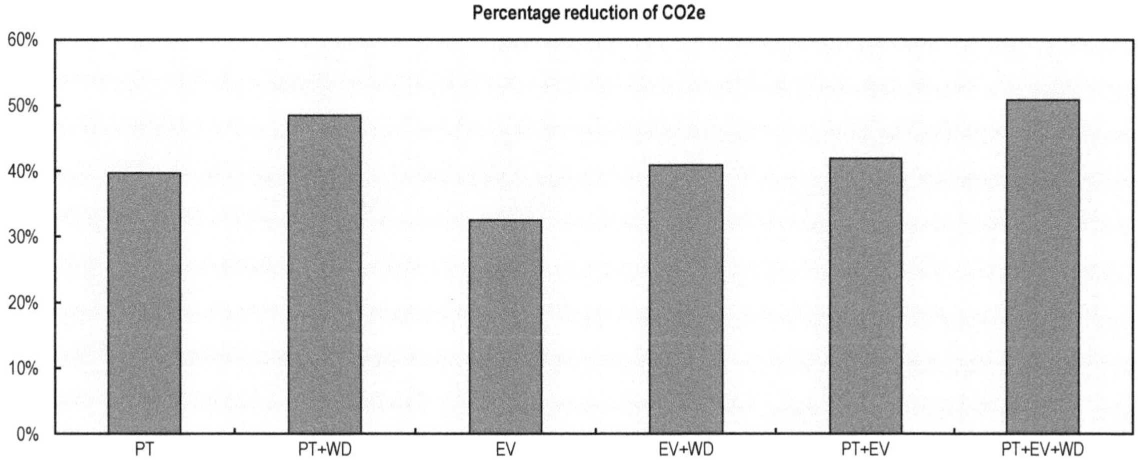

Note: PT refers to the "promote public transport" policy package; EV refers to the "promote electric vehicle" policy package; WD refers to a widespread densification program; TD refers to a targeted densification program; different combinations of the packages are denoted with '+'.
Source: Generated by the authors, using results of simulations from MOLES.

The "promote public transport" and "promote electric vehicle" policy packages change the shares of vehicle ownership and passenger-kilometres travelled by different types of vehicles. These results are reported in Table 5.2. Changes in vehicle ownership rates in response to policies remain moderate. This is due to the persistence of the non-modelled advantages of ICE vehicles over EVs (see subsection 5.2). The various disadvantages of public transport services also contribute also to the limited increase in EV ownership. In spite of this, the policy packages induce considerable changes in the share of passenger kilometres realised by public transport modes and EVs.

Table 5.2. Key modal split changes induced by the "promote public transport" and the "promote electric vehicles" policy packages

	Reference	PT	EV	PT + EV
% not owning a private vehicle	10.7%	13.8%	11.4%	12.9%
% km generated with public transport	7.6%	33.6%	20.8%	26.8%
% owning an EV	10.6%	10.6%	13.3%	15.1%
% km generated with an EV	11.3%	8.9%	17.4%	20.1%

Note: PT refers to the "promote public transport" policy package; EV refers to the "promote electric vehicle" policy package.
Source: Generated by the authors.

In addition to the changes reported in Table 5.2, the policy packages also affect the total distances travelled. All policy scenarios tested in the model significantly reduce the total passenger kilometres travelled. The main mechanism responsible for the reduction of passenger-kilometres in the "promote public transport" and "promote electric vehicles" packages is the presence of significant pricing measures. Combining widespread densification with a transport policy scenario reduces travelled distances even further while the relative shares of commuting, shopping and leisure trips do not change, as presented in Figure 5.21.

Figure 5.21. Split of total passenger kilometres by mode and trip category

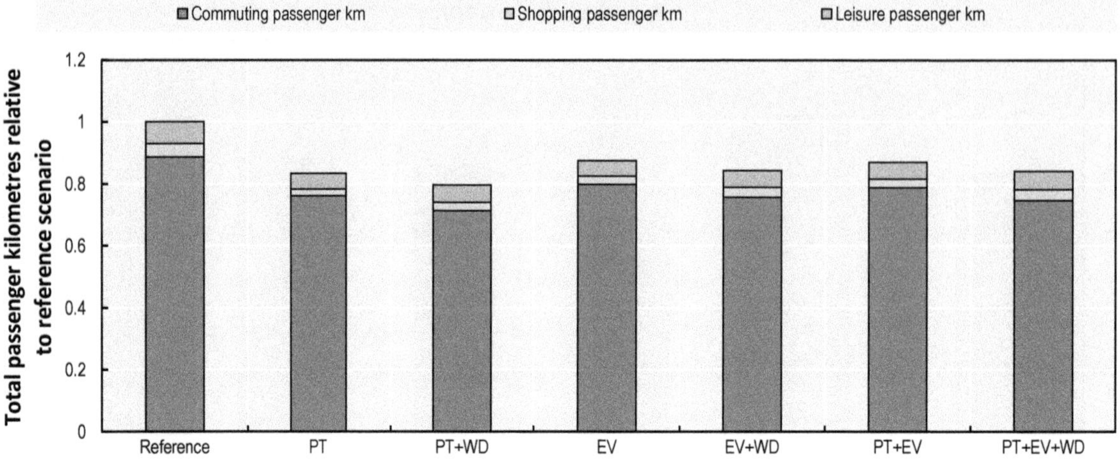

Note: PT refers to the "promote public transport" policy package; EV refers to the "promote electric vehicle" policy package; WD refer to a widespread densification program; different combinations of the packages are denoted with '+'.
Source: Generated by the authors, using results of simulations from MOLES.

The environmental effects of targeted densification packages, when these are combined with the "promote public transport" package, are displayed in Figure 5.22. All targeted densification packages provide significant additional cuts in transport CO_2e emissions. The largest cuts originate from combining the promotion of public transport with the "job-surrounding densification". The latter package is the densification program that induces an increase in the provision of housing supply in areas around the largest employment hubs. The associated reductions in passenger kilometres are shown in Figure 5.23.

An important finding of the analysis is the synergetic effect between targeted densification programs and the transport policy package. The multiplicative effect of targeted densification policies can be seen clearer by comparing: (i) the emission reduction potential of these packages as stand-alone policies and (ii) the additional emission reductions they generate when they are combined with the "promote public transport" package. For instance, the "job-surrounding densification" package (TD4) has the potential to reduce emissions from commuting by 6.7% as a stand-alone policy, but its contribution becomes much larger when it is combined with measures in the "promote public transport" package. That is, in the latter case it has a much stronger marginal effect, causing emissions to drop by more than 10%. A similar effect is found for the rest of the targeted densification packages. For example, the analysis shows that the "CBD-surrounding densification" package (TD1) causes emission reductions of 2.8% as a stand-alone policy and of 5% when it is combined with public transport support measures.

Figure 5.22. Emission reductions from promoting public transport and densification in the long run (2030-2050)

Estimated percentage of emissions eliminated in the long run by promoting public transport, with or without densification policies. The environmental effectiveness of displayed policies is considerably lower than in the mid-term. Percentage values are relative to emissions in the reference case in 2050.

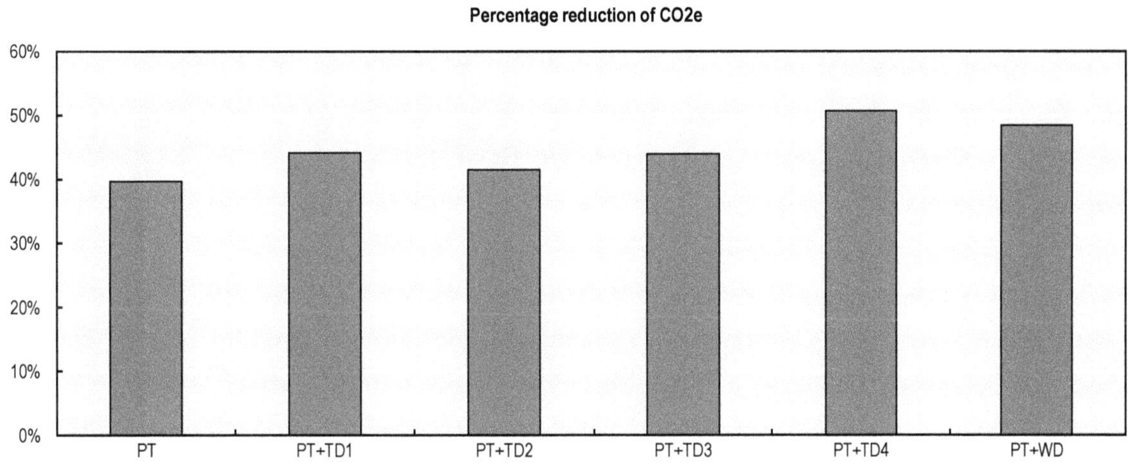

Note: PT refers to the "*promote public transport*" policy package; WD refers to a *widespread densification* program; TD refers to a *targeted densification* program; TD1 refers to further densification of already-dense areas lying close to major employment hubs and public transit nodes; TD2 refers to densification of low-density zones surrounding the central business district; TD3 refers to densification of low-density areas in Auckland's isthmus; TD4 refers to densification of areas in close proximity to employment hubs; combinations of the packages are denoted with '+'.
Source: Generated by the authors, using results of simulations from MOLES.

Densification decreases distances and thereby reduces travel time. In turn, this makes individuals more likely to respond to the price incentives the package incorporates. This is because as travel time falls, individual responses to price incentives become more elastic. Therefore, inducing people to switch transport modes is much easier than it would be, had the distances and travel times associated with public transport been longer.

The multiplicative effect of densification on the effectiveness of promoting public transport can be highlighted further with a closer look to the "job-surrounding densification" package (TD4). The analysis shows that densification around major employment nodes causes a non-negligible, but nevertheless limited increase (1.2 percentage points) in the share of kilometres undertaken by public transport. However, the same densification package causes the share of kilometres travelled on public transport to rise by 10.0 percentage points when this densification occurs alongside the "promote public transport" package. The reverse is also true: promoting public transport has a large effect in the share of passenger kilometres undertaken by public transport (26.0 percentage points) but that effect becomes even larger (34.7 percentage points) when TD4 is implemented. Similar findings can be reported for the rest of the densification policy packages.

Figure 5.23. Reduction in passenger-kilometres from promoting public transport and densification in the long run (2030-2050)

Estimated percentage of passenger kilometres reduced in the long run by promoting public transport, with or without densification policies. The environmental effectiveness of displayed policies is substantially lower than in the mid-term. Percentage values are relative to emissions in the reference case in 2050.

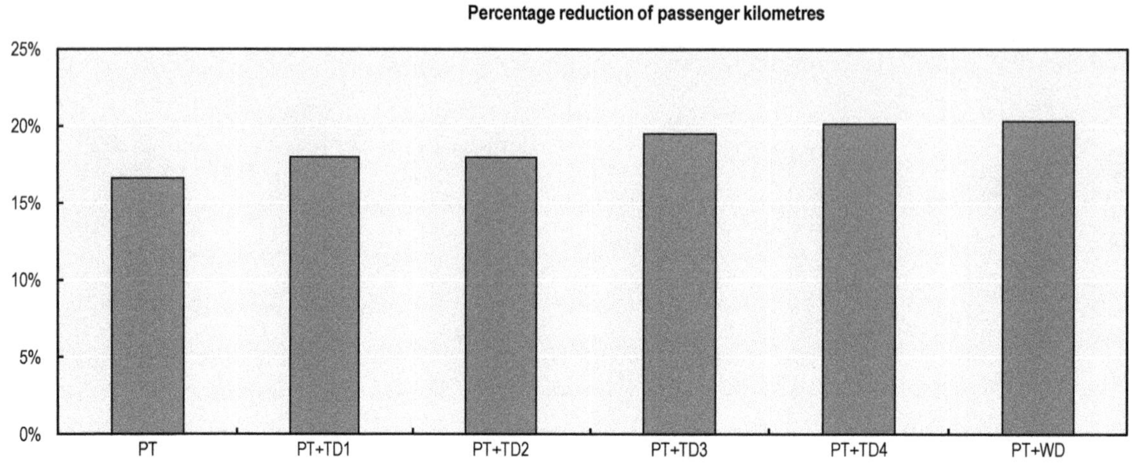

Note: PT refers to the "*promote public transport*" policy package; WD refers to a *widespread densification* program; TD refers to a *targeted densification* program; TD1 refers to further densification of already-dense areas lying close to major employment hubs and public transit nodes; TD2 refers to densification of low-density zones surrounding the central business district; TD3 refers to densification of low-density areas in Auckland's isthmus; TD4 refers to densification of areas in close proximity to employment hubs; combinations of the packages are denoted with '+'.
Source: Generated by the authors, using results of simulations from MOLES.

A large part of the environmental potential of densification may be undermined by strong and inelastic preferences for private open space (backyards). These preferences are relevant because a steep increase in building density implies a smaller amount of private open space (backyard) per unit of residential floor space. Therefore, when preferences for private open spaces are strong, densified areas become substantially less attractive. That increases the likelihood that a densification program will fail.

From an international viewpoint, the emission reductions induced by densification programs, as they are displayed in Figure 5.20 and Figure 5.22, can be seen as lower bounds in the decarbonising potential of these policies. This is because the preferences for private open space in New Zealand are particularly strong. The modelling exercise takes the structure of preferences into account, i.e. it assumes that large compensations are necessary to make up for any loss of private open space. As a result of that, all densification programs do not have the result that they would have in a context with more elastic preferences for private open space. The effect of weakening preferences for open space for the model results are tested in Chapter 6.

Finally, the modelling exercise understates the environmental potential of densification programmes, as jobs and facilities tend to follow the labour force. The reported results assume that the employment densities in the various locations evolve because individuals may change job locations. However, a more compact urban form would also induce jobs to move closer to the labour force. In turn, this would likely lead to a considerable decline in the kilometres generated by private vehicles in commuting.

5.3.6. Densification strategies and the housing market in the long run (2030-2050)

Figure 5.24. House price evolution

The evolution of house price index under the reference and counterfactual scenarios based on densification.

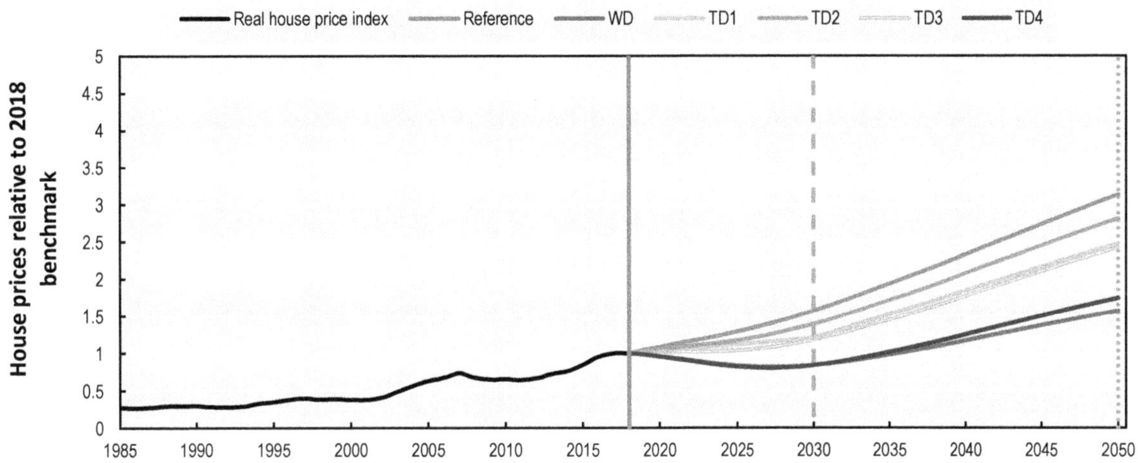

Note: TD refers to one of four targeted densification programs; TD1 refers to further densification of already-dense areas lying close to major employment hubs and public transit nodes; TD2 refers to densification of low-density zones surrounding the central business district; TD3 refers to densification of low-density areas in Auckland's isthmus; TD4 refers to densification of areas in close proximity to employment hubs; WD refers to a widespread densification program.
Source: Generated by the authors, using results of simulations from MOLES, (The Economist, 2019[3]).

Apart from facilitating the reduction of urban transport emissions, the various densification packages examined in the study are key to determining long-run housing affordability. Figure 5.24 displays the evolution of mean real housing prices from 1985 to the present, and the projected increase in these prices from 2018 to 2050. The historical data are based on numbers from The Economist (2019[3]), while the projections are results of simulations from MOLES.

Without a drastic policy intervention, the cost of housing in Auckland will continue growing along the current trajectory. The results of the reference scenario suggest that real house prices will be 60% higher by 2030 and at least 200% higher in 2050, compared to their levels in 2018. House price increases will affect all types of housing in a similar manner. Therefore, housing will become substantially more expensive in the long run.

The house price increases are likely to have a large distributional impact. Rising house prices benefits the segments of the population with a net positive income from rents to the detriment of renters with limited access to borrowing mechanisms.

For this reason, a widespread densification program is a necessary ingredient in a long-run policy response to the challenge of housing affordability. This type of densification has the potential to prevent housing prices from reaching levels that will cause further public discomfort. The simulations employed in the study show that widespread densification can limit real house price growth in the period 2018-2050 to 58%. That change lies slightly above the growth in the projected average income in New Zealand.

Targeted densification programs are the necessary intermediate steps between today's low-density urban form and a substantially more compact city in the future. Certain targeted densification programmes are welfare improving even in the short run, as shown in Figure 5.19. For example, introducing substantial densification in the isthmus area can limit the overall price growth until 2030 to 20%, i.e. much lower than the projected growth in the reference case, which is 60%.

The next subsection demonstrates that keeping housing prices on an affordable trajectory is key to long-run welfare.

5.3.7. The long-run welfare impact of policy packages (2030-2050)

The capacity of widespread densification to slow house price growth translates into substantial welfare gains. Reduced upward pressure on housing prices allows households to allocate spending to other areas, which increases welfare. The methodology used for the calculations of welfare impacts is detailed in Chapter 3.

The annual welfare gains of widespread densification amount to approximately 7.4% of income in 2050. This is the largest annual welfare gain computed by any policy or combination of policies in the study. Thus, addressing housing affordability through widespread changes to land-use regulations should be a key policy priority.

Figure 5.25. The long-run (2030-2050) economic impact of recommended land-use policies

The annual welfare gains or losses *per capita* from various densification programmes.

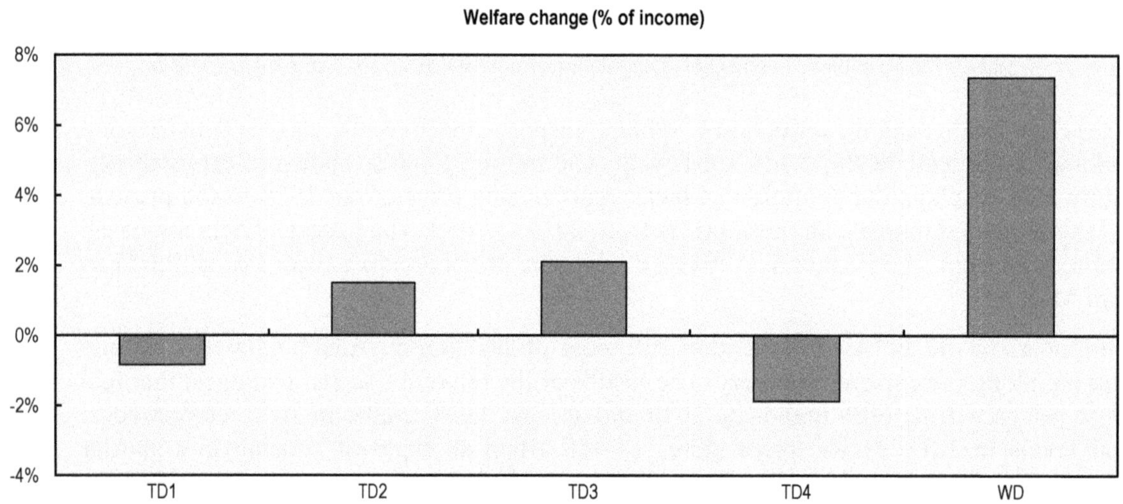

Note: TD refers to one of four targeted densification programs; TD1 refers to further densification of already-dense areas lying close to major employment hubs and public transit nodes; TD2 refers to densification of low-density zones surrounding the central business district; TD3 refers to densification of low-density areas in Auckland's isthmus; TD4 refers to densification of areas in close proximity to employment hubs; WD refers to a widespread densification program.
Source: Generated by the authors, using results of simulations from MOLES.

The transition to a more compact urban form is not likely to occur in a short time window. Rigid regulations, natural frictions in the transformation of a developed urban fabric and opposing views on the socially desirable urban development pattern will delay that process. Figure 5.25 shows that densification packages TD2 and TD3 generate substantial welfare gains, slightly below and above 2% of net income respectively. This implies that the welfare benefits from densifying the inner part of the urban area outweigh the losses from the decrease in the supply of private open space. Thus, a considerable part of the welfare gains of widespread densification can be seized with a targeted densification program. This programme would focus initially on the areas surrounding the central business district and subsequently on areas of low density within the isthmus area. However, restricting policy action to partial densification will not comprehensively address the issue of diminishing housing affordability, as the evolution of the housing market under different scenarios presented in Figure 5.24 suggests.

Figure 5.26. The long-run (2030-2050) economic impact of recommended transport policies

The annual welfare gains *per capita* from promoting public transport, EVs and both.

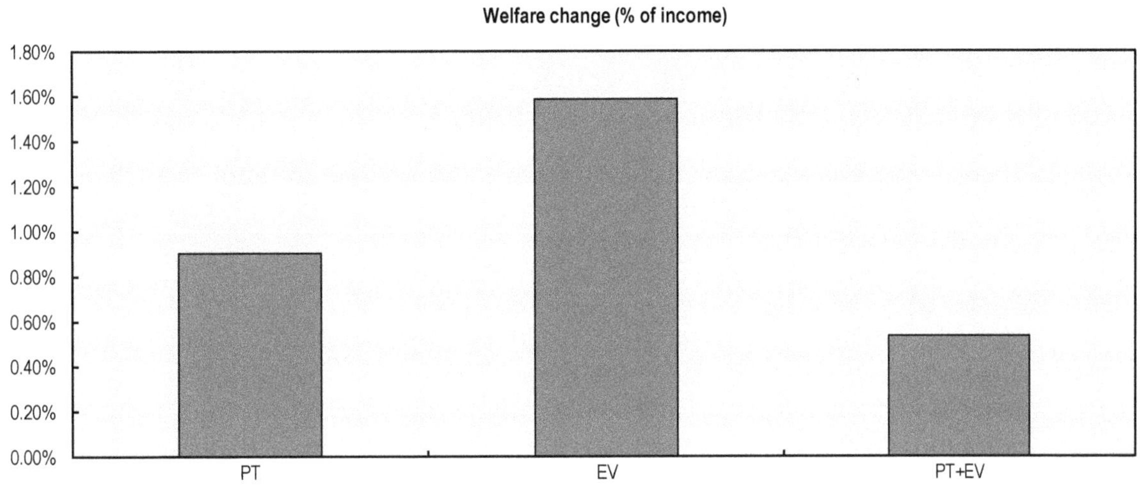

Note: PT refers to the "*promote public transport*" policy package; EV refers to the "*promote electric vehicle*" policy package; PT+EV refers to the combined implementation of the two policy packages.
Source: Generated by the authors, using results of simulations from MOLES.

The annual *per capita* welfare impact of transport policies is shown in Figure 5.26. Promoting public transport, electric vehicles or both will all generate considerable welfare gains in the period from 2030 to 2050.

Public transport subsidies incorporated in the "promote public transport" package could be more efficient in increasing the share of passenger kilometres travelled via public transport in the long-run than they are in the mid-term. This is because the non-modelled advantages that cars possess over public transport diminish by 2050, as shown in Figure 5.5.[2] However, the latter effect is outweighed by the increasing fuel efficiency of ICE vehicles.

5.3.8. Policy recommendations for the long run (2030-2050)

- **Implement a widespread densification program.** The simulations show that a widespread densification program will be effective in reducing greenhouse gas emissions and in curbing house price growth. In[3] spite of the strong preferences for open space, the model results indicate that a generalised relaxation of building heights and other density regulations will generate significant welfare gains.

- **Gradually increase the level of the fuel tax to offset the improvements in the fuel economy of ICE vehicles.** The level of the ETS component of the fuel tax should be aligned with the environmental objectives it serves. It could, for example, be linked to the average fuel efficiency of New Zealand's vehicle fleet, so that in the long-run that tax is automatically adjusted to offset the introduction of more fuel efficient vehicles.

- **Increase the flat kilometre tax, aligning it better with the increasing external costs of congestion.** Congestion externalities will very likely worsen over time. This is because a greater number of vehicles will be using the road infrastructure, which will not expand at the same pace. Furthermore, rising income implies a higher value of time. This means that every minute lost due to traffic will also have a higher social cost. Government can play a role by preparing the ground for tax instruments that will both offset an expected increase in congestion and charge the social cost of vehicle use to those using them. The existing kilometre tax is an example of such an instrument. It will have to be adjusted to match the cost of congestion and other traffic externalities more closely.

- **Increase public transport subsidies once the quality of public transport service has been substantially improved.** Public transport subsidies are more effective once the public transport system has been adjusted to improve service frequency, reliability and connectivity. Under these conditions, a switch from private vehicles to public transport can be achieved with relatively smaller public transport subsidies. That will be facilitated further by the emergence of a more compact urban form. The latter will increase public transport ridership and the occupancy rate in modes of public transport, which is currently low. In turn, that will further reduce the deficits of the public transport system. The study suggests that generous subsidies in public transport fares can be fully financed by the increase in the flat kilometre tax.

- **Further incentivise the switch to electric vehicles.** Direct and indirect subsidies to EVs will be more effective once the underlying technological differences between ICE and electric vehicles have been reduced. In the long-run, a flexible system of subsidies to EVs should be designed. Such a scheme should provide moderate subsidies, possibly financed by an increase in the annual ownership cost of ICE vehicles. However, the study suggests that such a scheme could have only moderate effects if the technological gap between the two vehicle types is not narrowed substantially.

- **Combine support for electric vehicles with public transport subsidies.** The EV subsidy scheme could also be combined with an active policy that promotes public transport in a way that minimises potentially antagonistic effects. For example, moderate EV subsidies could be provided in areas that will remain sparse and therefore hard to cover efficiently by public transport, while public transport subsidies could be higher for trips within a denser urban core.

- **Allow further expansion of the city only if future urban areas are well connected to the public transport system.** The social cost of future urban expansion will depend on whether future urban areas are well connected to public transport corridors and other forms of critical infrastructure.

Notes

[1] One of the study's limitations is that the fiscal costs of increased use of public transport are not considered in the welfare calculations. The implications of this are discussed in Chapter 6.

[2] That change represents an overall improvement in the public transport system of Auckland that cannot be explicitly modelled in the study. The planned infrastructure investments in transport suggest that this improvement will be sizeable.

References

Auckland Transport (2018), *Auckland's Low Emission Bus Roadmap*. [2]

The Economist (2019), *Global cities house-price index*. [3]

Tikoudis, I. and W. Oueslati (2017), "Multi-objective local environmental simulator (MOLES 1.0): Model specification, algorithm design and policy applications", *OECD Environment Working Papers*, No. 122, OECD Publishing, Paris, http://dx.doi.org/10.1787/151cf08a-en. [1]

Chapter 6. Beyond the case study: interpreting the findings and assessing their wider relevance

This chapter explores the degree to which the key policy recommendations of the study are relevant to contexts beyond Auckland and New Zealand. To that end, it revisits the projected reductions in greenhouse gas emissions and other key outcomes under different assumptions about the carbon intensity of the electricity generation sector, population growth and income evolution. Moreover, the chapter offers an extensive sensitivity analysis with respect to various model parameters including the evolution of preferences for open space, fuel efficiency, electricity and fuel prices, as well as of the pace at which advantages of conventional vehicles vis-à-vis electric cars fade out. That analysis identifies the factors that have an important impact on the key conclusions. Finally, the chapter enumerates a series of methodological limitations of the analysis and the impact they have on the key conclusions of the study.

6.1. Sensitivity analysis and external validity

This section assesses the extent to which the results presented in Chapter 5 are driven by the assumptions made about the evolution of exogenous variables. Population, income, the pre-tax purchase cost of vehicles and the prices of electricity and fuel are some of these exogenous factors. They play a key role in determining vehicle use, emissions, housing prices and other key outcomes of the model simulations. The reasons for which these variables are considered exogenous in MOLES are elaborated in Chapter 2. Conducting sensitivity analysis with respect to the exogenous variables is essential for two reasons.

Sensitivity analysis examines the *stability* of the main findings under alternative assumptions about the evolution of exogenous factors. That is, it enables to test whether the findings are *qualitatively stable*. In the context of this study, this means that the positive impact of various policies on emissions, welfare and other key outcomes remains positive, and *vice versa*. Qualitative stability also implies that the ranking of policies remain intact, i.e. the most socially desirable policies remain at the top of the list. Moreover, sensitivity analysis allows gauging the *quantitative stability* of findings, i.e. the extent to which their magnitude changes when the basic premises of the simulation exercise are altered. In the context of this study, policies induce welfare gains or losses, emission reductions or raises and budget surpluses or deficits. Sensitivity analysis helps to identify the background factors whose change causes the aforementioned effects to vary considerably.

Most importantly, sensitivity analysis is essential to gauge the degree to which the key findings and policy recommendations of this study are *externally valid*. That is, the analysis has a high degree of external validity if socially desirable policies identified for Auckland can be successful in achieving the same objectives in other urban areas. The sensitivity of the study's findings to its background premises is therefore key to advocate in favour or against the adoption of the policy recommendations included in this report by other cities that differ regarding these background factors.

6.1.1. Evolution of the attributes of electric vehicles

The assumptions regarding the pace of technological change in the EV industry are important for aggregate emissions. The model explicitly incorporates factors such as the purchase cost and the driving range of EVs. However, there is also a number of EV attributes, whose effect is modelled only implicitly. These attributes include, but are not limited to: charging time, the variety of EV models available and the cost of their spare parts. The evolution of such attributes matters for the take-up of EVs.[1]

The reference and counterfactual scenarios are simulated under a relatively pessimistic assumption about the evolution of these factors. More specifically, it is assumed that the advantage that ICE vehicles possess over EVs shrinks over time, but remains substantial until 2050. This assumption turns out to be important in determining the share of EVs in the vehicle fleet. In the reference scenario, that share remains modest through 2050. The share of households that own an EV in the model increases from 0.6% in the benchmark year to 10.9% in 2050. The "promote EVs" policy package increases this share to 13.1% by raising the pecuniary costs of owning and operating an ICE vehicle and by subsidising EVs. That difference is represented by the distance between the solid and the dotted line in Figure 6.1.

Adopting more optimistic view on the evolution of factors driving the advantage of ICE over EVs changes the picture considerably. Figure 6.1 shows that, under such view, the share of households that own an EV turns out to be 41.6% in 2050. This "alternative reference" scenario is represented by the long dashed line in Figure 6.1. It assumes that the various advantages of ICE vehicles *vis-à-vis* EVs disappear completely by 2050. The EV share in that alternative case can be increased further, from 41.6% to 46.8%, with the "promote EVs" policy package.

Figure 6.1. The share of EV ownership is highly influenced by assumptions about pace of technological change

The share of households that own an EV under different scenarios of technological development and policy intervention.

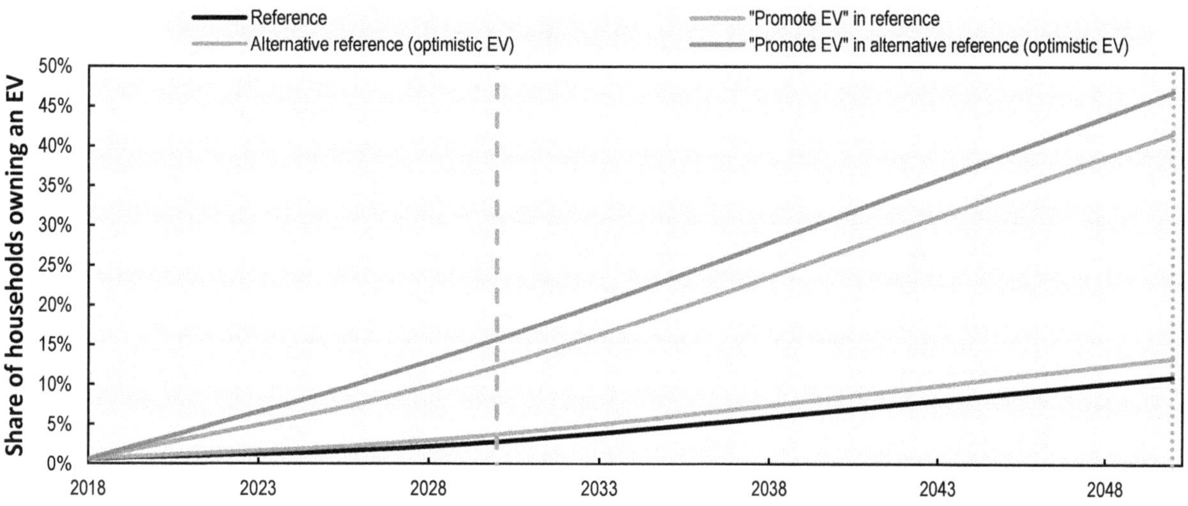

Note: Reference is the business-as-usual scenario; "Promote EV" in alternative reference reflects pessimistic assumptions about technological change and policies that support EVs over ICE vehicles; the alternative reference reflects more optimistic expectations of the pace of technological change but no new policies; "Promote EV" in alternative reference reflects optimistic expectations of technological change as well as policy support for EV uptake.
Source: Generated by the authors, using results of simulations from MOLES.

Figure 8.2 shows projected emissions to 2050 under various assumptions about EV attributes. The higher rate of EV penetration in the alternative reference scenario translates to substantial aggregate emission reductions compared to the original reference scenario. Emissions in the latter case increase by 6% between 2018 and 2050, as detailed in Chapter 5. In contrast, the alternative reference scenario that adopts a more optimistic view on the evolution of EVs yields a 30% decline in emissions during the same time interval (2018-2050). When the "promote EVs" package is implemented in combination with an optimistic view on the evolution of EVs, aggregate emissions fall by 64% in 2050 relative to 2018.

Figure 6.2. Optimistic expectations regarding the evolution of EV attributes and aggregate emissions

The evolution of aggregate emissions from urban transport in Auckland between 2018 and 2050 under different scenarios of technological development and policy intervention.

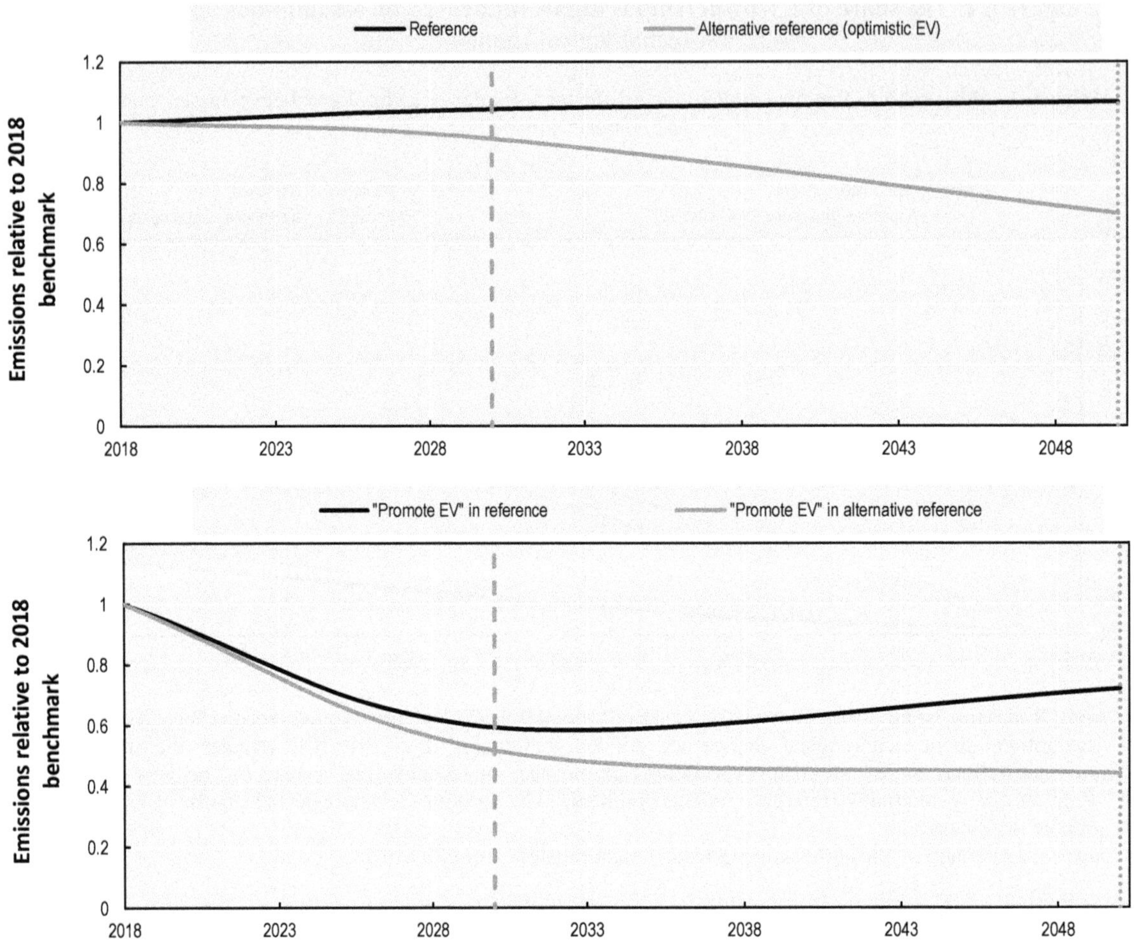

Note: The top panel depicts emissions in the original reference and the alternative reference scenario, which contains more optimistic expectations regarding the pace of technological change; the bottom panel displays the projected emissions under the implementation of the "Promote electric vehicles" package in the two reference scenarios.
Source: Generated by the authors, using results of simulations from MOLES.

6.1.2. Evolution of conventional vehicle fuel economy and grid carbon intensity

The study makes specific assumptions about the evolution of the GHG emissions per vehicle kilometre. For ICE vehicles, greenhouse gases are emitted directly from the tailpipe. Therefore, the emission intensity of ICE vehicle use depends on the fuel economy of the vehicle. For EVs, emission intensity is indirect: it depends on the electricity consumption per kilometre and on the carbon intensity of the electricity grid.

The evolution of ICE vehicle fuel economy is subject to uncertainty. On the one hand, the increasing share of hybrid cars, which have both an electric and an internal combustion engine, contributes to an improvement of their fuel economy. On the other hand, a decreasing investment in R&D that aims to improve the fuel economy of ICE vehicles contributes to keeping their fuel economy stagnant.

Improvements in the fuel economy of ICE vehicles lowers the fuel cost and therefore the per-kilometre cost of their use. The study assumes a 55.4% increase in the fuel economy (kilometres per litre) of ICE vehicles between 2018 and 2050. This makes ICE vehicles relatively cheaper to operate over time and hampers the switch to other transport modes.

Assuming no improvement in the fuel economy of ICE vehicles, aggregate GHG emissions from road transport are projected to increase by 60% between 2018 and 2050. That change, which is depicted by the solid black curve in Figure 6.3, has to be juxtaposed against the solid grey curve in the same figure. The latter displays the change in aggregate GHG emissions predicted by the original reference scenario over the same time period (6%). The dashed curves in the same figure indicate that the difference between the two scenarios is almost entirely due to the additional greenhouse gases ICE vehicles emit in the alternative reference scenario.

The sensitivity analysis displayed in Figure 6.3 provides useful insights on how urban transport GHG emissions could involve in contexts with lower fuel economy standards than those imposed in New Zealand.

Figure 6.3. Keeping conventional fuel economy fixed at its 2018 level significantly increases emissions from ICE vehicles

The evolution of aggregate emissions from urban transport and ICE vehicle emissions in Auckland between 2018 and 2050 in different scenarios of conventional vehicle fuel economy

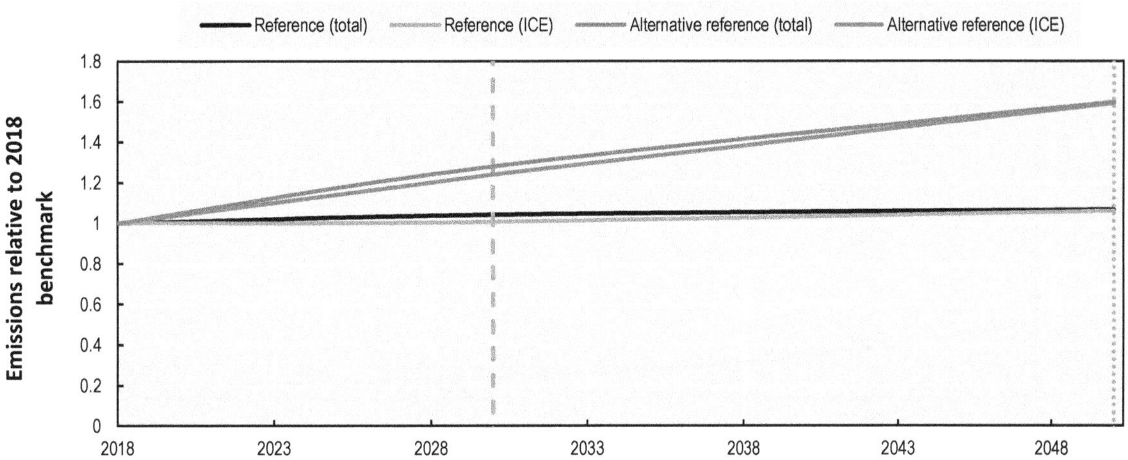

Note: All series in graph refer to the business-as-usual case. Reference is the total emissions from urban transport with improving fuel economy; Reference (ICE vehicles) charts emissions from ICE vehicles with improving fuel economy; Alternative reference is the total emissions from urban transport if fuel economy remains fixed at its 2018 level; Alternative reference (ICE vehicles) charts emissions from ICE vehicles if fuel economy remains fixed at its 2018 level.
Source: Generated by the authors, using results of simulations from MOLES.

The carbon intensity of New Zealand's electricity grid, which is significantly lower than in other countries, is the main driver of the low level of GHG emissions from EVs. A more carbon-intensive electricity grid results in higher GHG emissions per kilometre driven by EVs. Therefore, it hampers policies that promote EVs to reduce GHG emissions.2

The sensitivity analysis uses an alternative reference scenario, in which the carbon-intensity of the electricity generation sector is given by the global average value. This analysis allows revisiting the effects of policies examined in Chapter 5, in a world where electricity generation is much more carbon-intensive. In order to conduct this analysis, historical data from the IEA (2019[1]) are extrapolated to the period 2018-2050. This extrapolation generates an upper bound estimate of the average carbon intensity of the global electricity supply. This is presented in Table 6.1, alongside with the projected evolution of the carbon intensity of New Zealand's electricity supply. The latter is used in the original reference scenario, whose results are presented in Chapter 5. Using the upper bound values of carbon intensity results in higher GHG emissions per EV kilometre, as Figure 6.5 indicates.

Table 6.1. Projections of the carbon intensity of electricity

	Unit	2018	2030	2050
New Zealand	kgCO2e/km	0.119	0.057	0.022
World	kgCO2e/km	0.502	0.454	0.375

Source: IEA (2019[1]); authors calculations.

Figure 6.4. More carbon intensive electricity significantly increases the emission factors of EV

The evolution of the CO_2 emissions per kilometre under different assumptions about the carbon intensity of electricity

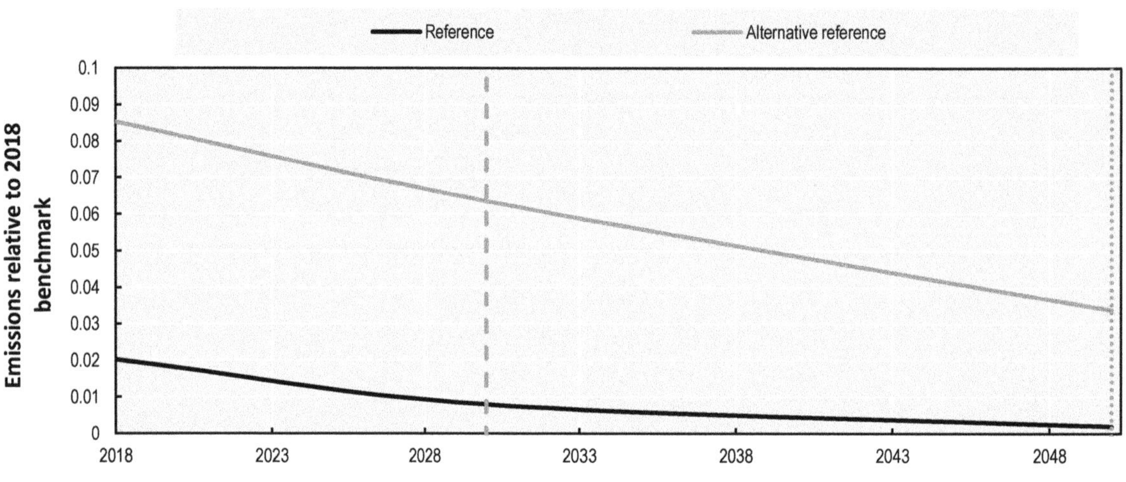

Note: Assumptions about EV electricity consumption per kilometre are detailed in Chapter 2 and kept fixed in this analysis.
Source: IEA (2019[1]) and authors' calculations.

Aggregate emissions increase from both EVs and public transport, particularly in the long run, when buses are projected to be fully electric. In the reference case, aggregate GHG emissions increase by 6% relative to the 2018 benchmark. In contrast, these emissions are 13% higher in 2050 than in 2018 with a more carbon intensive grid. This is displayed in the upper panel of Figure 6.5. The contribution of EVs and public transport in total GHG emissions increases as well. In the original reference scenario (clean New Zealand electricity grid), EVs and public transport are responsible for 5.4% of emissions in 2018. That number falls to less than 1% in 2050. In contrast, with a more carbon intensive electricity grid, EVs and public transport make up 8% of total emissions in 2018. That number falls only marginally in 2050, to 7%. This is displayed in the lower panel of Figure 6.5.

Figure 6.5. Higher carbon intensity of electricity increases aggregate emissions and the share of emissions from EVs and public transport

The evolution of aggregate emissions from urban transport and electric vehicles and public transport in different scenarios of carbon intensity of electricity

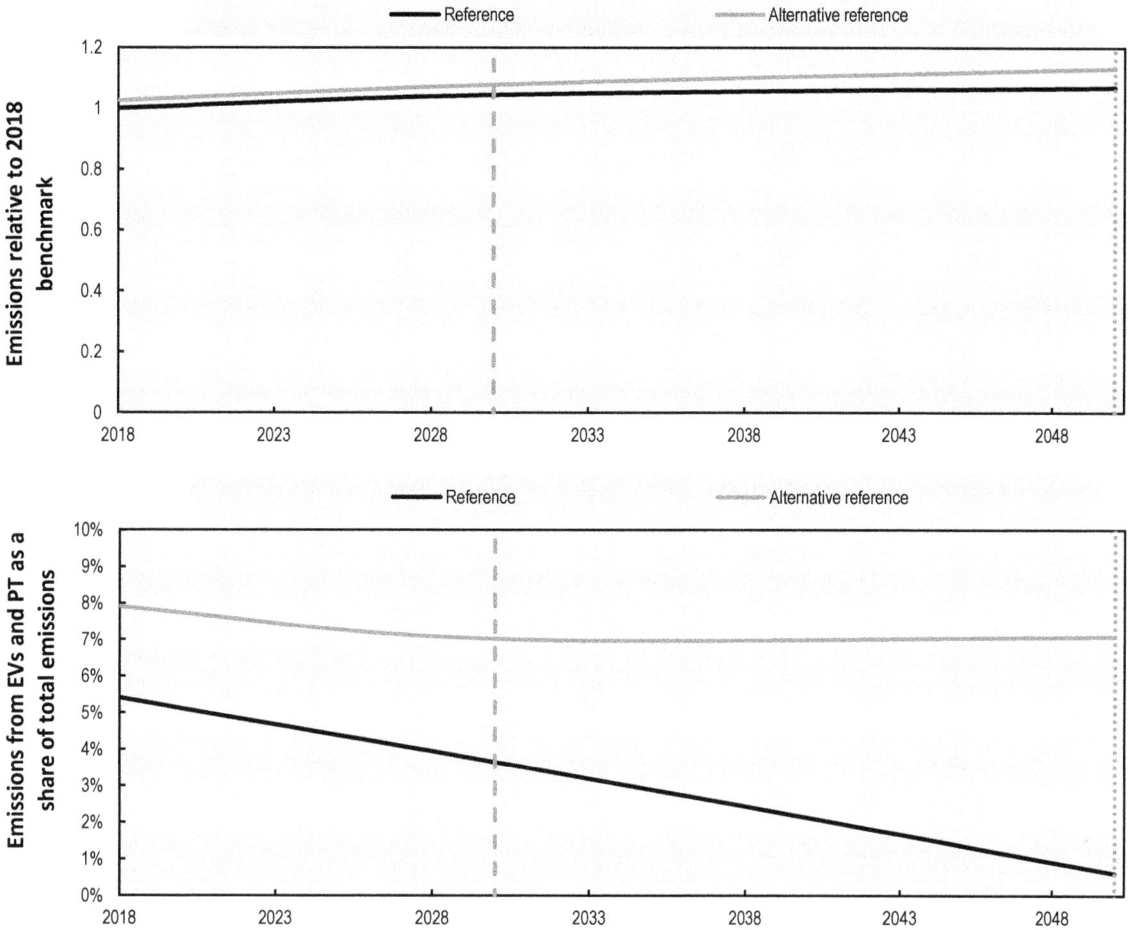

Note: Top panel displays aggregate emissions using the projections for the carbon intensity of the New Zealand grid (reference) and projections for the carbon intensity of a grid representative of average global carbon intensity of emissions (alternative reference); bottom panel displays the evolution of combined emissions from EVs and PT under different assumptions of carbon intensity.
Source: Generated by the authors, using results of simulations from MOLES.

6.1.3. Evolution of electricity and fuel prices

Electricity and fuel prices are two determinants of the operational costs of EVs and ICE vehicles. The original reference scenario Chapter 5 assumes that both electricity and fuel prices increase moderately between 2018 and 2050. The electricity price (NZD/kWh) increases by approximately 20% over the course of the study, while the fuel price (NZD/litre) increases by approximately 14%. These projections are based on extrapolations of historical data. For instance, the projection of electricity prices exploits the observation that, since 1980, these prices have increased on a yearly basis, with the exception of the period 2013-2017 where prices remained relatively stable.

A limitation of the study is that electricity prices do not depend on the penetration of EVs. However, higher EV adoption rates imply higher demand for electricity. That would require an increase of the total capacity of the electricity grid, or it could otherwise translate into higher prices. On the other hand, if electricity prices develop along the trend of the most recent years, prices will not increase and may even fall over time.

The analysis that follows explores the implications of deviating from the electricity price path assumed in the original reference scenario of Chapter 5. The alternative electricity prices, which can be considered as upper and lower bounds to the reference scenario, are presented in Table 6.2.

Table 6.2. Range of electricity prices simulated in sensitivity analysis

Variable	Unit	2018	2030	2050
Electricity prices used in the original reference and counterfactual scenarios	2017 NZD per kWh	2.31	2.68	3.07
Lower bound electricity prices	2017 NZD per kWh	2.31	1.34	1.53
Upper bound electricity prices	2017 NZD per kWh	2.31	4.02	4.60

Source: IEA (2018[2]); authors calculations.

Using the upper and lower bound of electricity price paths gives rise to alternative reference scenarios in which aggregate emissions do *not* differ substantially. Assuming that electricity prices evolve according to the lower bound path is associated with a marginal decrease (0.5%) in aggregate emissions. Similarly, assuming that electricity prices evolve according to the upper bound path is associated with an increase in aggregate emissions of a similar magnitude. This implies that electricity prices play a secondary role in predicting EV penetration rates.

Since price of gasoline affects the purchase and use of ICE vehicles, it is among the factors that determine aggregate GHG emissions. In New Zealand, that price has evolved in line with global oil prices in recent years. The projection used in the original reference scenario of Chapter 5 assumes a moderate increase of 14% in gasoline price between 2018 and 2050. The sensitivity analysis explores alternative scenarios for the evolution of gasoline prices. Upper bound and lower bound paths for the price are constructed as 50% higher and lower than the price in the original reference scenario, respectively. These are used in alternative reference scenarios, which are compared to the original reference scenario presented in Chapter 5. The resulting alternative price paths are shown in Table 6.3.

Table 6.3. Range of fuel prices simulated in sensitivity analysis

Variable	Unit	2018	2030	2050
Fuel prices used in the reference	2017 NZD per litre	0.97	1.11	1.21
Lower bound fuel price in alternative reference	2017 NZD per litre	0.97	0.55	0.61
Upper bound fuel price in alternative reference	2017 NZD per litre	0.97	1.66	1.82

Source: IEA (2018[3])

Changes in fuel price alter the attractiveness of ICE vehicles relative to EVs and public transport. Increasing the reference fuel price in 2050 by 50% reduces aggregate emissions by 2% relative to the reference case. That effect is roughly symmetric: decreasing the reference fuel price in 2050 by 50% increases aggregate emissions by 2% relative to the reference case. This is displayed in Figure 6.6.

Figure 6.6. Higher fuel prices lowers aggregate emissions, while lower fuel prices increase emissions

The evolution of aggregate emissions from urban transport under different fuel price levels

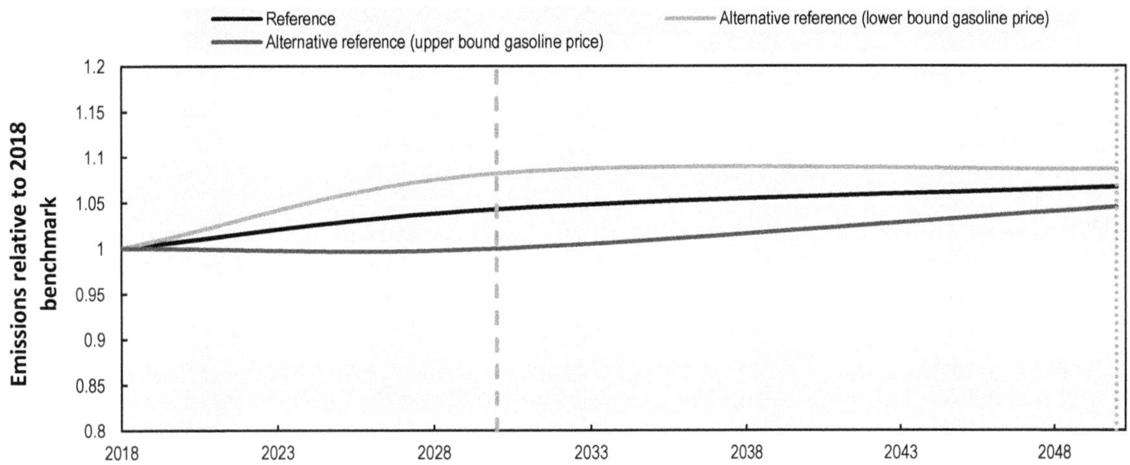

Note: Reference refers to the business-as-usual scenario; Alternative reference (Upper bound) simulates the evolution of emissions over time under higher fuel prices; Alternative reference (Lower bound) simulates the evolution of emissions over time under lower fuel prices. Fuel price ranges are presented in Table 6.3.
Source: Generated by the authors, using results of simulations from MOLES.

6.1.4. Evolution of income and population growth

Income and population are key determinants of GHG emissions in the study. Income bounds the expenditure capacity of individuals and shapes aggregate demand for housing, travel and various commodities. Population affects aggregate housing demand and therefore housing prices.

The original reference scenario of Chapter 5 uses the historical evolution of the *per capita* disposable income in New Zealand to extrapolate income growth (Statistics New Zealand,

2017[4]). The outcome of the projection is a real disposable income that grows steadily over time. Compared to 2018, it is 20% higher in 2030 and 54% higher in 2050.

To test the evolution of GHG emissions under alternative assumptions of income growth, income is kept fixed throughout the period 2018-2050. This slows the growth in aggregate GHG emissions, as emissions grow by 2% between 2018 and 2050 instead of 6%. This is displayed in Figure 6.7.

Figure 6.7. Keeping income fixed to its 2017 level reduces emissions relative to the reference case

The evolution of aggregate emissions from urban transport under different scenarios of income growth

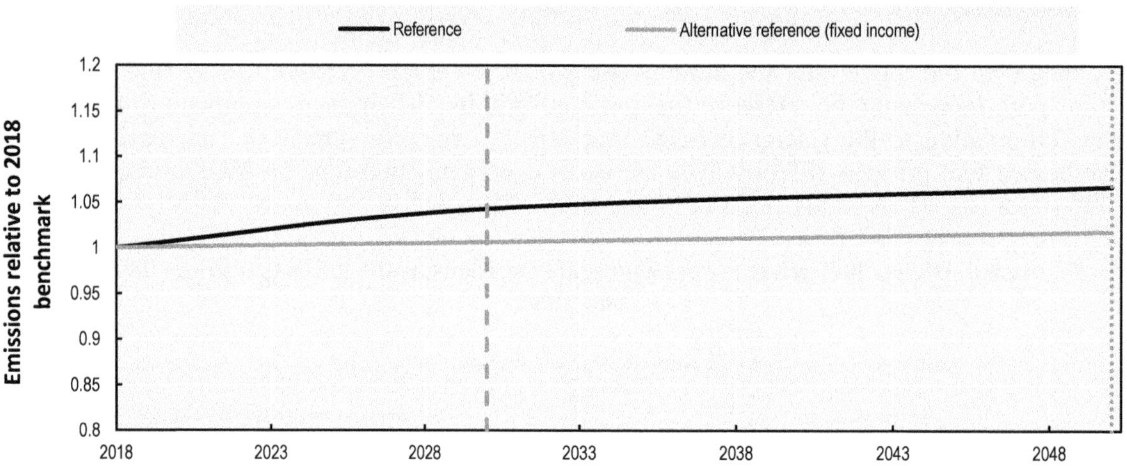

Note: Reference refers to the no new policies case; Alternative reference (Fixed income) keeps income fixed to its 2017 level.
Source: Generated by the authors, using results of simulations from MOLES.

Keeping income fixed alters the evolution of housing prices in Auckland considerably. Housing prices increase by more than 200% in the period between 2018 and 2050 in the original reference scenario examined in Chapter 5. In contrast, the alternative reference scenario, in which income is fixed, yields a much more moderate increase in housing prices. That is approximately 50%, as displayed in Figure 6.8. The juxtaposition of the original and alternative reference scenarios in that figure implies that a substantial part of the housing price increase is driven by real income growth.

Figure 6.8. House prices under different scenarios of income growth

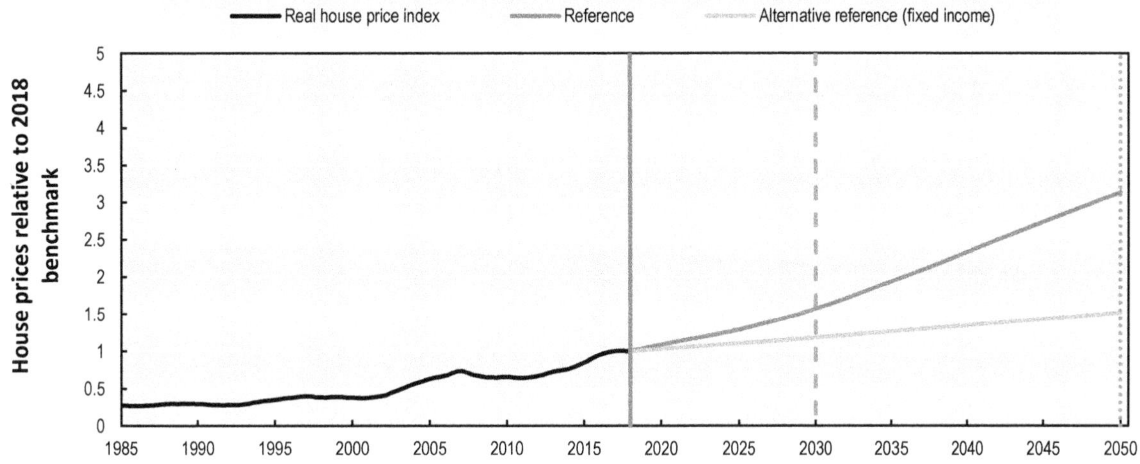

Note: Reference refers to the no new policies case; Alternative reference (Fixed income) keeps income fixed to its 2017 level.
Source: Generated by the authors, using results of simulations from MOLES.

Population growth has important implications for aggregate GHG emissions, as already discussed in Chapter 5. The projection of population used in the original reference scenario assumes that Auckland's population will grow by 75% between 2018 and 2050. However, there is substantial uncertainty regarding the rate of population growth in that long time interval. Therefore, two alternative reference scenarios are constructed using upper and lower bounds of population growth. The associated paths of population evolution are presented in Table 6.4.

Table 6.4. Population growth scenarios simulated in sensitivity analysis

	2018	2030	2050
Population used in study	1,300,000	1,690,000	2,600,000
Lower bound population	1,300,000	1,518,400	1,604,200
Upper bound population	1,300,000	1,604,200	2,282,800

Figure 6.9 displays the evolution of GHG emissions in the alternative reference scenarios that assume a lower and an upper bound for the evolution of population. If population growth is more rapid than assumed in the original reference scenario, aggregate GHG emissions in 2050 may be 20% higher than 2018. The population in this case will continue growing, in the entire period from 2018 to 2050, with the same pace observed during the last years. On the other hand, if population growth is slower than that assumed in the original reference scenario, GHG emissions in 2050 will be 15% lower than in 2018.

Figure 6.9. Emissions under alternative scenarios for population evolution.

The evolution of aggregate emissions from urban transport under different scenarios of population growth

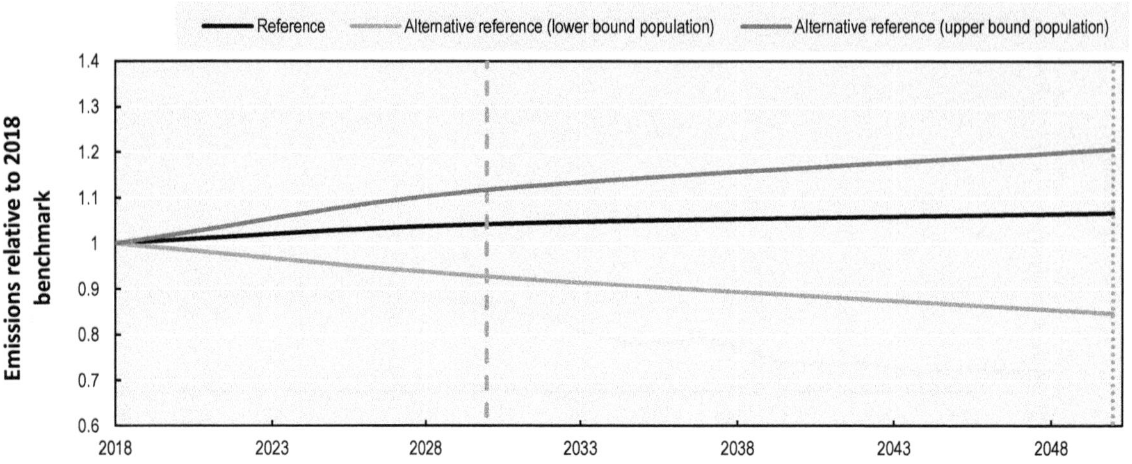

Note: Reference refers to the no new policies case; Low population uses the same assumptions but with more modest increase in population; High population uses the same assumptions but with a greater increase in population.
Source: Generated by the authors, using results of simulations from MOLES.

Like income growth, population growth has a significant impact on housing prices. Figure 6.10 displays the evolution of housing prices from 2018 to 2050 under the two alternative reference scenarios, which assume different population growth rates. If population growth is more rapid than what was assumed in the original reference scenario, real house prices in 2050 will be almost four times their level in 2018. On the other hand, if population growth is slower than expected, the associated increase will be approximately 110%.

Figure 6.10. House prices under different scenarios of population growth

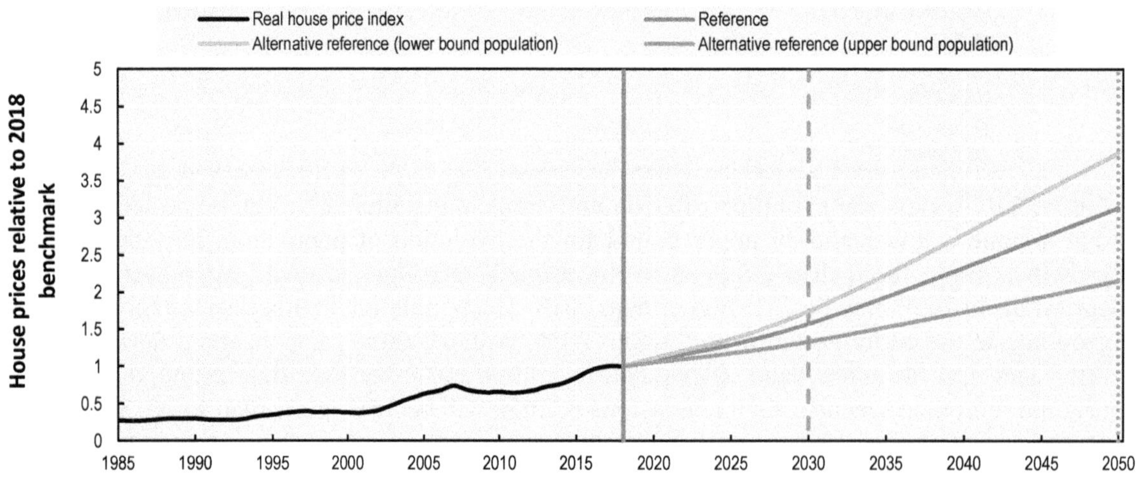

Note: Reference refers to the no new policies case; Low population uses the same assumptions but with more modest increase in population; High population uses the same assumptions but with a greater increase in population.
Source: Generated by the authors, using results of simulations from MOLES.

6.1.5. Sensitivity analysis of preferences for open space

The welfare impact of densification policies depends on whether private open spaces, such as backyards, are substitutes or complements to residential floor space. The original reference and counterfactual scenarios, which were examined in detail in Chapter 5, assume that the preferences for private open spaces are particularly strong in New Zealand. Under these scenarios, it is also assumed that residential floor space and private open spaces are strong complements. This means that household welfare increases with a larger home, but that increase is relatively small if it is not accompanied by an increase in private open space.

Assuming strong preferences for open space therefore implies that densification policies may lower welfare. The reason is that densification programmes increase building height and decrease the space between buildings. By doing so, such policies result in reductions in the amount of open space available for each unit of residential floor space. This may have a negative welfare effect, which could offset the positive welfare effect from the decrease in housing prices these programmes cause. This possibility is illustrated clearly in Table 6.5 and Table 6.6. Both tables show that certain densification programmes explored in the report cause welfare losses, when preferences for private open space are strong, as assumed in the original reference and counterfactual scenarios. The negative welfare effect of some densification packages is reversed in the long run, as the positive effects of reduced housing price growth offsets the detrimental effect densification has on individual preferences. It can also be seen that part of negative welfare effects of densification are mitigated when such policies are combined with the "promote public transport" package, which has a positive welfare effect *per se*.

This section conducts sensitivity analysis to identify the impact of the assumptions made on preferences for open space. More specifically, the analysis is based on an alternative reference scenario, in which the preference parameters that govern the demand for private open spaces are relaxed. The alternative reference scenario also relaxes the degree to which residential floor space and private open spaces are complements. The findings from applying the "promote public transport" and the various densification packages under weak preferences for open space are displayed in Table 6.5 and Table 6.6.

Table 6.5. The welfare impact of densification policies

The welfare effect of stand-alone densification packages, when preferences for open space are strong or weak

	2030		2050	
Preference for private open space	Strong	Weak	Strong	Weak
Widespread densification	-0.62%	3.84%	7.36%	14.31%
Transit-oriented densification	-4.10%	-2.06%	-0.83%	2.13%
CBD-surrounding densification	0.23%	1.46%	1.50%	3.16%
Isthmus densification	-1.01%	1.51%	2.11%	5.63%
Job hub-surrounding densification	-9.50%	-5.87%	-1.87%	3.84%

Note: Welfare impacts are expressed as percentages of net income.
Source: Authors' calculations based on outcomes from MOLES.

Table 6.6. The welfare impact of combining densification policies with the promotion of public transport

The welfare effect of various densification packages combined with the "promote public transport" package, when preferences for open space are strong or weak

	2030		2050	
Preference for private open space	Strong	Weak	Strong	Weak
Widespread densification	0.78%	5.11%	7.37%	13.52%
Transit-oriented densification	-2.84%	-0.92%	0.09%	2.65%
CBD-surrounding densification	1.28%	2.40%	2.21%	3.64%
Isthmus densification	0.26%	2.70%	2.80%	5.91%
Job hub-surrounding densification	-7.86%	-4.30%	-0.94%	4.15%

Note: Welfare impacts are expressed as percentages of net income.
Source: Authors' calculations based on outcomes from MOLES.

Both tables suggest that a substantial shift in preferences causes the welfare effects of various densification packages to improve. This is intuitive as densification brings about a smaller welfare loss if preferences for open space are weaker. The most profound change is that widespread densification, combined with a promotion of public transport, turn out to be the optimal policy response even in the mid-term. The reason for this is that under weak preferences for open space, well-being is primarily determined by housing affordability. This can be verified by comparing welfare impact of the "CBD-surrounding densification", the "Isthmus densification" and the "Widespread densification". The sequence of these packages gradually generalises densification from the inner core of the city to the entire urban area. When preferences for private open space are weak, the welfare-enhancing effect of densification increases with the area of the city in which the densification program applies. This is because densification attenuates house price growth over a larger area of the city.

Furthermore, when preferences for open space are weak, all densification packages are welfare-improving in the long run. This is in sharp contrast with the case of strong preferences for open space, in which some of the densification packages are detrimental even in the long run.

The analysis is relevant for contexts outside New Zealand, where preferences for open space may be weaker. It can also provide insights about alternative outcomes in the long run, as it can be argued that a shift away from strong preferences for low density could be possible, even in New Zealand.

6.2. Limitations of the study

6.2.1. Limitations stemming from assumptions about exogenous variables

The conclusions reached in this report depend on concrete hypotheses about the evolution of factors that the model has no predictive power over. These factors include population, income, the energy efficiency of vehicles, the carbon intensity of the electricity generation sector and the prices of fuel and electricity. The assumptions about the intertemporal evolution of these factors were elaborated in Chapter 2. The impact of these assumptions on the key outcomes of the study are examined in the previous section, which provides extensive sensitivity analysis. That analysis expands the validity of several findings to other settings. These may resemble Auckland in some respects, for example in urban morphology, but differ in others. For instance, the first part of this chapter has shed light to the case of a sprawled city of comparable characteristics, such as population and income, where electricity is produced in a more carbon-intensive way. That analysis is therefore relevant for several urban areas in Canada, the United States and Australia.

6.2.2. Limitations stemming from model specification

The external validity of the analysis, *i.e.* the extent to which the findings of the study can be widely generalizable to contexts outside Auckland, is to some extent limited by the spatial configuration of the model. The latter is elaborated in Chapter 3.

The study used a *medium resolution*, stylised representation of the spatial layout and the actual transportation networks. This resolution is higher than the usual degree of detail in scientific work, where multiple abstractions are necessary to derive insights about the properties of policies in generic contexts. For instance, the road networks in this study are represented by hundreds of nodes and links. Similarly, urban development is represented by hundreds of residential zones. Therefore, the spatial resolution of the model closely mirrors the actual spatial layout of the city, reflecting in detail its unique geographic characteristics.

Consequently, the recommendations of the study are to some extent specific to Auckland. The exact degree to which the spatial specificities of Auckland drive the reported results is unknown. That degree could be identified in an analysis that would remove all idiosyncratic characteristics of the urban area from the spatial configuration of the model. These include, but are not limited to, the large water bodies and the isthmus area that characterize Auckland. Thus, that analysis requires generic hypotheses about spatial structure. Insofar such an exercise is feasible, it goes beyond the scope of this study. It is therefore left as a topic of future research.

Nevertheless, it the main policy conclusions of the study are generally robust in the context of the specific spatial configuration used in the model. Repeating the modelling exercise with a more generic network and spatial configuration would alter the results of the study from a *quantitative* viewpoint. For instance, it can be argued that without the water bodies, overall private transport costs in the city would be lower. In turn, that would affect the share of income allocated to transport. It would also affect housing prices, which are affected by accessibility. However, it is unlikely that the findings of the study would change *qualitatively*, as the analysis keeps the spatial and network configuration fixed across the reference and the various counterfactual scenarios. Therefore, that configuration is not affected by policy changes.

On the other hand, the model abstracts from explicitly modelling a series of local, particularly idiosyncratic characteristics. These features may bear some relevance in the context of Auckland, but that relevance is very limited to other contexts. One of the most important idiosyncratic characteristics is the existing set of regulations regarding volcanic view shafts. These are spatially refined land-use regulations that aim to protect the visibility of volcanoes from various locations. Explicitly accounting for such characteristics would shift the focus away from deriving overall recommendations for optimal land use and transport policies. Instead, such an approach would direct the focus to how these optimal policies should be modified in order to fit the various local idiosyncrasies. The latter adjustment is left as a task to policymakers in New Zealand. The overarching messages of this report should be read in the context of the various local constraints.

Another important abstraction adopted in the modelling exercise is that the location of employment hubs is fixed throughout the entire horizon of the study. This implies that job locations do not respond directly to the policies examined in the study. However, the model still mimics the real-world dual response of households and jobs to changes in accessibility. That is, in MOLES an increase in the pecuniary cost of private vehicle use creates incentives for individuals to relocate closer to their workplace or to pursue a job in an employment hub that lies closer to their residential location. This implies that the density of employment, i.e. the number of workers employed at different locations, is also endogenous.

It can still be argued, however, that the indirect ways in which employment responds to policy changes in MOLES do not capture the full relocation effects these policies may trigger. To the extent that this is valid, the report underestimates the actual welfare benefits of the examined policies. This holds true because firms tend to move closer to location of labour. The policies examined in the study, especially densification policies, create compact urban forms. Therefore, they generate incentives for some of the firms located in peripheral job hubs to move to the inner part of the city, where a larger share of the labour pool resides. Insofar these incentives are not offset by an increase in land rents in central areas, which these firms also have to face, job relocation reinforces the positive effects of household relocation.

Another limitation stems from the choice to avoid modelling the provision of public transport services in an explicit way. The latter choice would substantially increase the computational burden as the behaviour of the various transport providers and authorities would have to be specified and fit into the model. Instead, MOLES uses fixed coefficients to convert passenger kilometres in public transport to rail and bus vehicle kilometres. Some of the examined policies in the report drastically increase passenger kilometres, causing a proportional increase to the kilometres traversed by buses and trains. Therefore, the findings do not account for the substantial part of these additional passenger kilometres in public transport that can be accommodated only through an increase in occupancy rates in buses and trains. A similar argument holds for the way passenger kilometres in public transport are converted to greenhouse gas emissions from public transport vehicles.

An immediate outcome of that is that the model *underestimates* the potential of the various policies examined in the report to reduce congestion and emissions. The most profound case is the policy package entitled "promote public transport", which causes the largest change in the private-to-public transport passenger kilometre ratio. The impact of the policy on emissions and congestion is large, but the estimates get even larger by revisiting some of the model's assumptions. For instance, someone can argue that the frequency of public transport service does not have to increase proportionally to bus and rail passenger kilometres, as the study assumes. Instead, most of the additional demand for public transport services will be absorbed by the current activity of public transport modes. This argument is particularly strong for Auckland, where existing occupancy rates are relatively low, but can apply to other contexts where public transport is far from being the dominant mobility option.

The above underestimation of emission reductions is much smaller in 2050. This is because the emission intensity of public transport vehicles declines steadily with time and is projected to be very low in 2050. Therefore, underestimating the potential of policies to reduce traffic in the long run implies a smaller bias in the estimation of their potential to reduce emissions.

The operational costs of public transport are affected by the policy packages examined in the report. That holds particularly true for the "promote public transport" policy package, which induces a massive change in the modal split in favour of public transport modes. The potential impact of such policies on the existing deficits of public transport operators should also be taken into account by local policymakers.

The counterfactual scenarios in the study did not consider the impact of a large investment in public transport infrastructure. Such an investment could considerably increase the capacity and frequency of service and might prove more cost-effective than the large fare subsidy included in the "promote public transport" package. The study does not explore this possibility due to lack of stated- or revealed-preference data on the way that individuals respond to public transport attributes such as frequency, comfort and reliability.

Finally, the model adopts the standard approach of general equilibrium models to individual preferences, assuming that these are fixed over time. This approach is necessary in order to identify the true effect of policy interventions and price shocks on individual behaviour and economic outcomes. Keeping preferences constant may be perceived as a general limitation of equilibrium models. However, that assumption is essential in order for all of the outcomes of the simulation outcomes to be attributed entirely on the policy shocks that generate them.

6.3. Beyond the study: additional considerations and future extensions

The study exclusively considers the impact of land use and transport policies on exhaust emissions and emissions from the production of the electricity used to charge electric vehicles. Well-to-tank emissions (i.e. emissions from extracting, producing and transporting fuel) are not within the scope of emissions considered. It should be stressed that the policy packages explored in this study do not affect that latter category of emissions.

Unlike the estimates for *tank-to-wheel* emissions, the expansion of the study to a full-blown lifecycle analysis is a more challenging task. This is because the policies in the report affect the ratio between EVs and ICE vehicles and because the carbon footprint in the production stage differs between these two vehicle types. In particular, several studies find that EVs arrive on the market with a higher carbon footprint than ICE vehicles, as the production of their battery is energy-intensive (Wu et al., 2018[5]; Ellingsen, Singh and Strømman, 2016[6]).

The report focuses exclusively on emissions from mobile sources. These emissions arise from fossil fuel combustion and the electricity used to power EVs, electric buses and rail. However, the policy reforms examined in the report, especially those involving densification policies, alter the structural density of urban development. There is preliminary evidence in the literature that structural density is related to the energy consumption of buildings, as their energy needs for cooling and heating depend, among others, on the way urban development is organised across space. Future extensions of this study may examine the degree to which the policies examined in this report increase or decrease the amount of greenhouse gas emissions that can be attributed to static sources.

The policies examined in study could generate broader benefits that are not explicitly considered in the analysis. For example, a shift towards low-carbon transport improves air quality and reduces noise. These benefits are not included in the welfare calculations. Additionally, the health benefits of a shift towards active modes of travel such as biking or walking are not considered.

The different policies tested eliminate only a part of aggregate greenhouse gas emissions from urban transport. Further reductions require policies that promote research and development (R&D), in order to increase the pace of technological progress in key areas relevant to the transport sector. Computing the social cost and benefit of such R&D policies goes beyond the scope of this report, as such policies are mainly relevant in EV-manufacturing countries.

Other technological developments, such as shared mobility and autonomous vehicles, can have a direct effect on the trajectory of transport sector emissions. In a series of case studies, the International Transport Forum (ITF) assessed the likely impacts of shared mobility and found that a shift to shared autonomous vehicles has the potential to dramatically lower emissions and congestion (ITF, 2015[7]; ITF, 2017[8]). These possible developments are not addressed in the scenarios presented here. Incorporating different forms of mobility (e.g. shared mobility, micromobility) into the analysis would require future extensions of the current study.

The approach taken in this report can be a springboard to explore the impact of other urban policies on the economy and the environment. It can also be a point of departure for similar work that examines different environmental implications of land use and transport policies. In line with these extensions, future work may assess possible synergies or trade-offs between reducing greenhouse gas emissions and tackling air pollution, or focus on the effect of policies aiming to promote more energy efficient housing.

Notes

[1] See Chapter 5 for more details on how the relative advantage of ICE vehicles over other modes of transport gradually declines over time.

[2] This assumption does not affect the modal split between ICE vehicles and EVs. That is because the price of electricity is not linked to the use of EVs and, therefore, their emissions.

References

Ellingsen, L., B. Singh and A. Strømman (2016), "The size and range effect: lifecycle greenhouse gas emissions of electric vehicles", *Environmental Research Letters*, Vol. 11/5, p. 054010, http://dx.doi.org/10.1088/1748-9326/11/5/054010. [6]

IEA (2019), "Emissions per kWh of electricity and heat output", *IEA CO2 Emissions from Fuel Combustion Statistics* (database), https://dx.doi.org/10.1787/data-00432-en (accessed on 20 August 2019). [1]

IEA (2018), *Energy prices in national currency per unit.* [3]

IEA (2018), *Energy prices in national currency per unit.* [2]

ITF (2017), "Transition to Shared Mobility: How large cities can deliver inclusive transport services", *International Transport Forum Policy Papers*, No. 33, OECD Publishing, Paris, https://dx.doi.org/10.1787/b1d47e43-en. [8]

ITF (2015), "Urban Mobility System Upgrade: How shared self-driving cars could change city traffic", *International Transport Forum Policy Papers*, No. 6, OECD Publishing, Paris, https://dx.doi.org/10.1787/5jlwvzdk29g5-en. [7]

Statistics New Zealand (2017), *Disposable income per person*, http://archive.stats.govt.nz/browse_for_stats/snapshots-of-nz/nz-social-indicators/Home/Standard%20of%20living/disp-income-pp.aspx. [4]

Wu, Z. et al. (2018), "Life cycle greenhouse gas emission reduction potential of battery electric vehicle", *Journal of Cleaner Production*, Vol. 190, pp. 462-470, http://dx.doi.org/10.1016/j.jclepro.2018.04.036. [5]

www.ingramcontent.com/pod-product-compliance
Ingram Content Group UK Ltd.
Pitfield, Milton Keynes, MK11 3LW, UK
UKHW051505290926
15471UKWH00008B/1422

9 789264 903227